SUCCESSFUL AGING

Mary O'Brien, M.D.

Biomed General
Concord, California
© 2007

SUCCESSFUL AGING

P.O. Box 272007
Concord, California 94527-2007
USA

925-288-3500 (tel)
925-680-1201 (fax)
info@biocorp.com

Author
Mary O'Brien, M.D.

Managing Editor
Barbara Boughton

Cover Design
David Bailey

Illustrations and Layout
Shellane Holgado
Rex Salazar

ISBN 1-893549-14-3

This book is not designed to substitute for professional medical advice. Always consult a medical professional before making major changes in eating habits or taking supplements.

To obtain more information about Biomed General's products and services, please contact us at the above address.

ABOUT THE AUTHOR

Dr. Mary O'Brien (M.D.) is board-certified in internal medicine and geriatrics and has served on the medical school facilities of Georgetown University and the University of North Carolina. She is also a board-certified Physician Nutrition Specialist. She frequently lectures to health professionals on infectious diseases, women's health issues, pharmacology, and nutrition.

ABOUT BIOMED GENERAL

Biomed General is an organization that provides health care professionals with the latest scientific and clinical information. Biomed's live seminars and home–study courses are designed to help health professionals provide better care for their patients. Biomed General operates nationwide in the United States as well as internationally.

Biomed General
P.O. Box 272007
Concord, California 94527-2007
USA

925-288-3500 (tel)
925-680-1201 (fax)
info@biocorp.com

DEDICATION

This book is dedicated to my parents,
Hugh & Emma,
who have been the secrets of my success.

Dr. Mary O'Brien

Table of Contents

PREFACE

It's inevitable. Everyone will age; in fact we all get a little older each day. Unfortunately, aging is a process that's neither appreciated nor revered in today's youth-oriented society. Though aging does mean a few wrinkles and stiffer joints, it also brings benefits, including wisdom, insight and time to pursue one's favorite passions.

As we get older, we often spend our time pursuing "aging cures"—eye lifts, wrinkle-reduction surgery and hair dyes—all in an effort to prevent or reverse the aging process. But staying as young as possible in spirit, appearance and physical health often means simply living well. That may mean slowing down the frenetic pace of our lives, looking for ways to make lemonade out of life's lemons, or taking on healthy habits like exercise that improve the quality of our lives.

When you look at aging as an opportunity to expand your horizons, it all begins to sound a lot more pleasant. It's a time unmarred by the worries of youth—a time for enjoying retirement, travel, family, and personal relationships. And contrary to stereotype, it's both a time to savor life and engage in interesting new activities.

Everyone ages, but some people seem to age more happily and healthily than others. The "secrets" that follow are a collection of the wit and wisdom of people who have aged successfully.

Some of the "secrets" are profound and others are simply based on good old common sense. Many of these healthy habits have been recognized for centuries while others are the result of recent scientific research. Most of them require daily practice. Fortunately, the payoffs in health, well–being, and just plain fun make their daily practice worth it.

Ideally, this book should be used as checklist of good habits to recommend to your patients. It really doesn't matter if you're 19 or 90, the "secrets" in this book will help your patients look and feel better now and in the years to come.

CHAPTER 1
AGING WELL IS YOUR CHOICE

As a man thinketh, so is he, and as a man chooseth, so is he.

–Ralph Waldo Emerson

None of us can choose how long we will live. Even the healthiest lifestyle can't guarantee a long life. We can, however, choose how well we will live. That's a bold and powerful concept because it requires us to accept responsibility for the quality of our lives. This does not imply that sufficient doses of positive thinking will prevent bad things from happening. Bad things happen to good people all the time. Illness, loss, tragedy, and stress are part of the human condition.

What we can control and help our patients to control is our attitude or response to life's upsets and disappointments.

American culture does not treat the aging process kindly. In fact, growing old is viewed by many as life's biggest disappointment. Negative myths and stereotypes about older individuals abound.

Words used to describe old people often include "slow," "sad," "bitter," "mean," "stodgy," "sour," "boring," "dull," and "depressing." Small wonder so many people are terrified of growing old.

> IT WOULD TAKE THREE MILLION PAID FULL-TIME WORKERS TO PROVIDE THE SAME LEVEL OF ASSISTANCE PROVIDED BY SENIORS.

Many people see growing older as a time of chronic illness and disability. But this belief is one of the biggest myths about old age. Even in advanced old age, an overwhelming majority of seniors have little functional disability, and only about 5% live in nursing homes.

Another common myth is that ill health keeps many older people from being productive. Yet one-third of elders work for a living, one–third serve as volunteers in hospitals, churches and community organizations, and many seniors provide crucial assistance to sick and disabled family members, friends and neighbors. In fact, it would take three million paid full–time workers to provide the same level of assistance provided by seniors.

The alternative to growing old is not appealing. Very few people look forward to a premature death. The only sensible solution is to choose to age successfully. Perhaps as more and more people make that choice, words like "happy," "enthusiastic," "dynamic," "loving," and "fun," will describe a new image of old age.

| WHAT IS SUCCESSFUL AGING? |

It's not the years in your life but the life in your years that counts!
–Adlai Stevenson

Successful aging is not about having the face and body of a 20–year–old when you're 110. Barring manipulations of DNA, that's simply not possible, and it's probably just as well.

It would undoubtedly be exhausting. Successful aging is simply enjoying the maximum quality of life at any given age.

Waking up every morning to the sound of birds singing, fixing your own breakfast, and going out for a walk may not represent the height of excitement to many 20-year-olds, but most 90-year-olds would consider it a good deal. That's a fairly straightforward example, but on closer examination it contains one of the most important secrets of successful aging. People who age successfully spend a lifetime appreciating and enjoying the little, simple pleasures other people overlook—a beautiful flower, a walk in the woods, or the sound of the birds singing in the early morning.

The ability to experience pleasure is a hallmark of successful aging. But pleasure doesn't really exist unless we're conscious of it. To a large extent, we all create our own reality. If I fail to notice a breathtakingly beautiful sunset, that sunset doesn't become part of my reality. No matter how gorgeous it may be, I can't experience pleasure from it until I'm actively aware of it. The bad news is that we all miss hundreds of opportunities to experience pleasure every day.

The good news is, we can train ourselves to be far more perceptive and appreciative.

Successful aging has many facets but perhaps none is as vital as having a purpose in life. But, your purpose in life goes far beyond your profession. Many people tend to describe or define themselves by what they do. In fact, "What do you do?" is usually the second question we ask people after, "What's your name?"

> SUCCESSFUL AGING HAS MANY FACETS BUT PERHAPS NONE IS AS VITAL AS HAVING A PURPOSE IN LIFE.

This is usually not a significant problem until retirement. But then it can result in a bona fide identity crisis. When you've spent the last 40 years identifying yourself as a banker, nurse, accountant, teacher or business executive, retirement can mean a sudden drop in self–esteem. Nobody wants to be just "another retired old guy."

Without a clear sense of purpose in life, though, that's precisely what many older people become. Successful agers know why they're here.

They have a reason for living, a mission in life. They have a contribution to make to the people they love and the world in which they live.

| You Can't Pick Your Parents |

The Role of Heredity
With him for a sire and her for a dam/
What should I be but just what I am?
–Edna St. Vincent Millay

Some people live to 100 smoking cigars and eating platefuls of high fat meals. They're probably blessed with the sort of protoplasm that can withstand more than a few indiscretions along the way. Yet even the hardiest DNA can succumb to repeated environmental assaults. To put it more bluntly, unhealthy habits can foul up even the greatest genes.

On the other hand, someone with a family history of early heart attacks before age 50 could consider it a victory to reach retirement. For these patients living long will require a consistently healthy lifestyle as well as a bit of good luck.

No one really understands the precise role heredity plays in the aging process. Certain disorders such as heart disease, diabetes, hypertension and cancer can run in families and cause premature death. But family members generally share many environmental exposures, habits and lifestyles.

What is certain is that heredity is not as strong an influence on health as many believe. Research tells us that environment and lifestyle have a significant impact on the risk for all but the most strongly genetic illnesses, such as Huntington's disease. Exercise, diet and some medications can all delay or reduce the likelihood of developing a disorder.

So it's probably wise to align ourselves with the ancient Greeks who opted for "moderation in all things." Unless startling scientific studies reveal otherwise, maintaining a balanced, healthy lifestyle sprinkled with a few special treats is key to a healthy old age.

| CHOOSING A LIFESTYLE: HEALTHY IS HAPPIER |

Our happiness depends on wisdom all the way.
—Sophocles

Personal integrity demands a confession here. I have had and occasionally revert to an outrageously unhealthy lifestyle consisting of far too much stress, far too little exercise, and embarrassing quantities of chocolate. I learned,

> THE ONLY WAY TO MAINTAIN GOOD HEALTH OVER A LIFETIME IS TO HAVE ENJOYABLE HABITS THAT HAPPEN TO BE HEALTHY.

or rather, continue to learn my lesson after nearly losing my health permanently. I doubt I'll ever be a health food nut or fitness fanatic, but I do try to follow the same advice I've given patients over the years. And, I'm delighted to report it works wonders.

Diets don't work and exercise programs often fail because sooner or later we stop. Boredom, stress, work, or fatigue sneak into our lives and before long, diet and exercise sneak out. The only way to maintain good health over a lifetime is to have enjoyable habits that happen to be healthy.

People who truly love running or swimming or biking usually get their exercise because they need it to be happy. If the thought of jogging in 30–degree weather does not bring a sparkle to your eyes, you'll probably find a superior reason not to do it. I know, I'm always too busy to jog in 30–degree weather.

Similarly, people who love fresh fruit have actually been known to consider it dessert. This is a strange concept for those of us who are chocoholics. But you get the point.

Watching TV while eating potato chips and dip is many people's idea of a fun activity. But a more creative approach to health is more helpful—and fulfilling. Stop for a minute and think of all the enjoyable activities that are healthy. A walk in the park, a bicycle ride or ballroom dancing all qualify as healthy activities. Would some juicy grapes or a handful of almonds hit the spot? These are foods necessary for good health. Experts advise sneaking in a few healthy pleasures every day.

Before long these healthy pleasures can add up to happiness—and a life free of chronic disease and disability.

| You're Never Too Young to Start Aging Well |

They live ill who expect to live always.
—Publilius Syrus

No one grows old overnight (except for a few pathologic variants). And yet, we try desperately to avoid thinking about old age until it's upon us. That's unfortunate because aging is a cumulative process. The cigarettes and sun exposure and inactivity and frowns of a lifetime leave their mark in old age. The best (if not only) way to age successfully is to start as a child.

A lifetime of healthy, balanced living and positive attitudes is easy to spot in someone who's 80 or 90 years old. Its absence is equally obvious. The "secrets" that follow can benefit teenagers and retirees alike. Aging well is not a matter of luck. Aging well is a choice.

2

CULTIVATING A YOUTHFUL ATTITUDE

It is the disposition of the thought that altereth the nature of the thing.

—John Lyly

Attitude truly is everything when it comes to successful aging. We all know at least a few individuals who consistently look and act 10, 15, or even 20 years younger than they really are. Without exception, such inspiring people have a vibrant, youthful attitude. They're fun to be around and for the most part, other people don't think of them as "old."

Folks who have aged prematurely dominate the other end of the spectrum. Frequently their appearance has been battered by unhealthy habits such as smoking, heavy drinking, over–eating, and sun exposure. But almost always, they have a cynical, negative attitude that sends most people running in the opposite direction. They can be described quite accurately as sour old poops.

No one wakes up one morning thinking, "Gosh, I think I'll become a sour old poop!" But negative, pessimistic, bitter thoughts tend to multiply quickly. They spread insidiously, much like cancer cells. Before long they can destroy a person's well being as completely and efficiently as any disease.

Older people who have a "sour old poop" attitude are, in fact, at risk for ill health. In a study of 659 middle–aged and older men by Harvard researchers, published in the Annals of Behavioral Medicine, those who had the most optimism had higher levels of general health perceptions, vitality, mental health and lower levels of bodily pain. Depressive symptoms were associated with reduced levels of functioning in many domains. So an optimistic attitude can help seniors improve their attitude as well as improving their health.

OPTIMISTIC ATTITUDE CAN HELP SENIORS IMPROVE THEIR ATTITUDE AS WELL AS THEIR HEALTH.

| OVERCOME THE FEAR OF AGING AND DEATH |

Do not fear death so much, but rather the inadequate life.
−Bertolt Brecht

It seems wonderfully ironic, but the most successful agers don't give a hoot about aging or death. They don't count every new wrinkle or gray hair and they certainly don't fret about each approaching birthday. They enjoy the present and, just as important, they look forward to the future.

This is no small feat in a culture that worships youth and engages in collective handstands to avoid any thought of mortality. Paradoxically, the people who have acknowledged and accepted their own mortality are the ones who live life to the fullest day in and day out. Fortunately, accepting your own mortality does not mean living in constant dread of it as one woman explained, "We couldn't wait to move to Florida and join a senior care community. But now we're having second thoughts.

People sit around griping about growing old, and a major form of entertainment is checking out the obituary column every day. It's like living in heaven's waiting room, only it's beginning to feel like hell."

Many retirement communities are far more active and pleasant, but the scenario she describes is not a rare one. Over the centuries numerous philosophers have observed that people create or attract the very things they dread. The best way to ensure a miserable old age and unhappy death is to worry about it on a regular basis.

| IGNORE SOCIETY'S EXPECTATIONS |

Society is always taken by surprise at any new example of common sense.
–Ralph Waldo Emerson

When "The Golden Girls" premiered in 1985 people all over the country sat up and took notice. The sweet, silent, sexless stereotype of little old ladies was shattered almost overnight. Americans were not accustomed to "women of a certain age" being feisty, assertive, sensuous, and dynamic. Some people were appalled. Most applauded.

Unfortunately, many older individuals are still intimidated by society's expectations. They don't want to look foolish or silly by failing to "act their age." Sadder yet are some adult children who pressure their older parents to conform to their image of "respectable" old age. The thought of Mom or Dad enjoying a romantic interlude in their 60s or 70s is enough to send some adult children running for commitment papers.

Interestingly enough, the real masters of successful aging don't pay the slightest attention to society's expectations of aging. If they want to start a second or third career at 70, they do it. (Grandma Moses never picked up a paint brush until she was 76.) If they want to go back to school or travel across Europe or get married at 80, they do it. Such actions invariably raise an eyebrow or two but more often than not, it's out of jealousy.

Slowly the negative stereotypes are fading. Nolan Ryan outshined pitchers half his age. Audrey Hepburn set a standard for elegance that younger stars can only aspire to. And older folks in business, science, education, and the arts are breaking new ground daily, giving their younger colleagues some stiff competition.

So just as it's important to take your patients' blood pressure, it may be crucial to encourage them to talk about and live their dreams, as much as possible. Special challenges and exciting adventures can truly make life worth living.

| BECOME INTERESTED AND INTERESTING |

I am never bored anywhere: being bored is an insult to oneself.
–Jules Renard

Boredom afflicts most of us from time to time. By mid–July many school kids complain they have nothing to do. Retirees facing a perpetual weekend often wonder how they'll fill the time. Some find boredom difficult to admit, but it's surely not difficult to recognize. A bored person is not a lot of fun. Youthful, dynamic people of any age are interested in the world around them.

Usually, they're positively fascinated by one or more particular areas of interest. They love or at least enjoy their work. (It's almost impossible to age well if you hate your work.) And they can't wait to learn something new.

If you have a patient who's been feeling bored or lonely lately, you might be able to help by giving him or her this little quiz of "interest index."

INTEREST INDEX	YES	NO
1. I enjoy my daily routine or work.	___	___
2. I have a hobby I pursue regularly.	___	___
3. I enjoy reading.	___	___
4. I love learning new things.	___	___
5. I appreciate the fine and performing arts.	___	___
6. I keep up with current events.	___	___
7. I enjoy talking to people from different backrounds.	___	___
8. I update my skills periodically.	___	___
9. I interact with people of all ages.	___	___
10. I love a good challenge.	___	___

Tell your patients to tally up the "yes" responses and check his or her "interest index."

WHAT THE SCORES MEAN

10 You're a sharp cookie and people probably enjoy your company.

7 – 9 You've got an interesting life and with a little push it could be great.

3 – 6 You're feeling a little dull around the edges – get moving before you lose another minute.

0 – 2 You need to make a major shift in your life. Begin pursuing the things that truly interest you.

Dale Carnegie once observed that we tend to like the people who like us. Similarly, the best way to interest others is to take an interest in them. The results can last a lifetime.

| MAKE ENTHUSIASM A WAY OF LIFE |

Nothing great was ever achieved without enthusiasm.
–Ralph Waldo Emerson

Enthusiasm is contagious. So is a lack of it. Over a lifetime, the presence or absence of enthusiasm may well be the single most important determinant of success, and may play a part in our overall health. Even our most intense efforts can fall flat without the sparkle of enthusiasm.

Successful agers know this. Whether they're baking a cake or building a corporation, they give it their best shot. Of course, enthusiasm comes easily when everything is going well. The trick is maintaining that zest and zeal when you're tired or broke or bored. But the folks who manage to do precisely that over a lifetime leave a trail of truly great accomplishments.

There is one little catch here. It's awfully tough to be enthusiastic in a vacuum, or worse, around a bunch of confirmed pessimists. Remember, you don't want to catch other people's lack of enthusiasm. The best solution is to seek out people who are energetic, optimistic, and enthusiastic, and encourage one another.

Another good way to beef up your enthusiasm is to tell others of our accomplishments. That's why seniors often gain so much from journal writing and telling the stories of their lives to others. Encourage your elder patients to tell tales of their life accomplishments either by talking to others or journaling, and pass on their knowledge to others. Studies tell us that journaling and telling life stories is a good way for seniors to recognize their triumphs, gain self-knowledge, and look forward to new adventures with enthusiasm.

| EXPECT THE BEST |

It's a funny thing about life:
If you refuse to accept anything but the
best you will very often get it.
—W. Somerset Maugham

Almost everyone is familiar with the concept of the self-fulfilling prophecy. Convince yourself of something and it will probably come to pass. It can be something wonderful or dreadful, the principle is the same. The power of belief is very real and it can be harnessed to transform a drab existence into a dazzling adventure.

Many people expect old age to usher in loss, loneliness, illness, and incapacity. And that's precisely what they get. Not that serious problems can be wished away, but dwelling on problems is an uncanny way of attracting even more of them.

No one understands how the subconscious works but, rest assured, it does work.

Why let your subconscious work against you when, with a little guidance, it can work wonders? So how do you guide the subconscious? Simple. You talk to it—a technique often taught in cognitive behavioral therapy.

We all talk to ourselves a hundred times a day when we think, "Gosh, I can't believe I did that. I'm such a klutz!" or "How could I have left the stove on. I'm so stupid!" Somewhere, deep down, all these little thoughts are registered, and the process starts in early childhood!

It may help to advise your patients to learn to give themselves regular mental pep talks. It's not silly. Professional athletes, actors, business magnates, and successful people in every field do this constantly, because it works.

Your patients can tell themselves they're strong, capable, and happy, or beautiful, energetic, successful, and smart—whatever are the qualities they most need to emphasize. The truth is that people can become what they repeatedly tell themselves they are.

This "secret" of self–talk, practiced consistently over 20, 30, or 40 years, can enable people to have an old age that is active, exciting, abundant, and happy. As a wise man observed long ago, "You may not always get what you want, but you'll usually get what you expect." And that's a good reason to expect the best.

| LAUGH — A LOT |

Laughter is a tranquilizer with no side effects.
–Arnold Glasow

When was the last time you had a good, hard belly laugh? You know, the kind that makes your sides hurt. Stop for a minute and remember how you felt afterward. Did you feel tense, tired, or irritable? Probably not, in fact, I'll venture to say definitely not.

Laughter is a tool your patients can utilize for good health, and to just feel good.

Laughter, in fact, has some extraordinary effects on our physiology. It forces us to fill our lungs more deeply and improves oxygen levels in the blood. It causes the blood pressure and pulse to go up a bit and then come down significantly for as long as an hour. And it reduces secretion of adrenalin and cortisol, the so—called stress hormones. If someone concocted a drug that did this much they could retire a billionaire tomorrow.

It really is true that laughter is the best medicine.

CHAPTER 3

How to Make the Most of the Body You've Got

The first wealth is health.

—Ralph Waldo Emerson

Unfortunately, there are no shortcuts to good health. I know. I've looked for them. But taking good care of your body doesn't have to be a grind. It can actually be quite enjoyable once you get the hang of it.

Most advice on diet and exercise is offered by people who are obsessive–compulsive on the subject of fitness. I clearly am not among their ranks. I believe fitness regimens should be fun and feasible and fit for normal human beings who occasionally crave a hot fudge sundae. With that in mind, the following "secrets" of successful aging, practiced regularly, can help people make the most of the body they've got.

| LEARN TO LIKE EXERCISE |

I felt compelled to get this one out of the way first, because, quite frankly, I hate exercise. I have, however, learned to incorporate more aerobic activity into my life without joining a gym or taking out a second mortgage to pay for running shoes.

Ideally, everyone should engage in aerobic activity for 30 minutes, most days to keep a healthy heart. Most people need to work up to this level and if they're over 50 or have any problems such as diabetes or heart disease they should consult their doctor first.

Even the most sedentary souls can usually begin a walking program. Walking outdoors is most relaxing but when the weather is rough, mall walking will do nicely. Your patients may want to consider bicycling (easy on the joints) or swimming. Actually, water exercise is fabulous for people with arthritis, muscle diseases, or weakness after a stroke.

> IDEALLY, EVERYONE SHOULD ENGAGE IN AEROBIC ACTIVITY FOR 30 MINUTES, MOST DAYS TO KEEP A HEALTHY HEART.

Of course, one should never be alone in a pool, lake, or ocean.

Dancing is a superb form of aerobic exercise. It's great fun and can do wonders for your social life as well. Those who don't have a dance partner can always pull the drapes and dance alone or consider the oriental dance/exercise/meditation of Tai Chi. It really can't be considered aerobic, but it's an excellent way to improve balance, coordination, and gracefulness. Yoga is another good option.

QUICK TIP FROM DR. O

THERE ARE DOZENS OF WAYS TO GET MORE EXERCISE WITHOUT CHANGING CLOTHES OR BUYING SPECIAL EQUIPMENT. CONSIDER THE FOLLOWING EXAMPLES:

1. TAKE THE STAIRS WHENEVER YOU CAN.

2. PARK A FEW BLOCKS AWAY AND WALK.

3. WALK WHEN YOU PLAY GOLF.

4. MOW YOUR OWN LAWN (WALK DON'T RIDE).

5. SPEND AN HOUR WITH A TWO-YEAR-OLD (OKAY 20 MINUTES).

6. USE A HAND MIXER INSTEAD OF AN ELECTRIC ONE.

7. WASH YOUR OWN CAR (AND SAVE TEN BUCKS).

8. GO SHOPPING.

9. TURN OFF THE TV AND DO ANYTHING.

10. MAKE LOVE.

A 2001 study published in the Journals of Gerontology found that an extensive literature review of large population-based studies revealed that even moderate level physical activity may provide protection from chronic disease. So regular participation in activities such as walking, climbing stairs, biking or gardening—which increase energy expenditure and maintain muscular strength, should be encouraged in older adults.

Another study published in the Journal of the American Geriatric Society in 2001 followed 5,888 subjects over 65 years old for seven years. Those who were free of chronic disease at baseline were monitored for onset of cancer, heart disease and fatal outcomes. As it turned out, physical activity was one of the most important behavioral factors for maintaining good health, according to the researchers.

Learning to like exercise starts with being less passive and more active. It's absolutely vital to anyone who wants to age well. If there's any tenet of the aging process that's inescapable, it's this one: use it or lose it.

| EASE UP ON ALCOHOL |

A glass of fine wine now and then can be a true pleasure. But the ill effects of alcohol consumed on a regular basis are numerous. Many people find they fall asleep more easily after a drink or two but they may be restless or wide–awake at 2:00AM. Although alcohol is really a depressant, it can stimulate the reticular activating system in the brain, wreaking havoc with sound, restful sleep. The problem often worsens with age. So if insomnia is a concern, steer clear of alcohol for a while and see if things don't improve.

Several studies have shown that the daily consumption of 2 drinks can help reduce the risk of coronary artery disease. However, the adverse effects of alcohol on the liver, pancreas, esophagus, stomach, immune system, and bone marrow must be weighed against possible benefits to the heart. An alcohol dementia syndrome involving confusion, memory loss, poor coordination and balance has been described in recent years and is not limited to skid row alcoholics. It's being diagnosed with greater frequency in "respectable" people who simply have "a few drinks every day."

The prudent course is to ease up on alcohol if you drink every day. There's no need (for most people) to become teetotalers but your body will do better over the long haul if you save the bubbly for special occasions.

| Make Tobacco Taboo |

Smoking and successful aging are mutually exclusive. A few heavy smokers linger into their 80's and 90's despite tobacco's ill effects. But they rarely feel well and they certainly don't look good. Far more numerous are the smokers who battle heart and lung disease in their 30's, 40's and 50's.

Any substance that adversely affects blood vessels as much as nicotine does is an enemy of successful aging. By damaging the endothelium or lining of blood vessels, nicotine causes narrowing and erosion of arteries, which accelerates arteriosclerosis and aggravates high blood pressure. Heart attacks, strokes, and peripheral vascular disease are frequently the end result. Bronchitis and emphysnema plague smokers as do frequent colds, upper respiratory infections, and pneumonia. Cancers of the face, mouth, esophagus, lungs, kidneys, and bladder are far, far more common in smokers than nonsmokers.

Not surprisingly a study in the Journal of the American Geriatric Society found that one of the best ways to ensure a healthy old age was to refrain from smoking. And this association held true even after controlling for cardiovascular disease risk factors and subclinical disease in the study participants, all over age 65.

All in all, smoking is an expensive way to guarantee a sickly, premature old age and a most unpleasant demise. Smoking also causes deep, premature wrinkles that are decidedly unattractive. On top of that it smells awful and wastes money. Some good advice for your patients: Make tobacco taboo.

| CUT DOWN ON CAFFEINE |

All across the world, millions of people count on caffeine for a jump-start in the morning. And many drink it morning, noon, and night, without apparent adverse consequences. But many people do become more sensitive to the stimulant effects of caffeine as they get older. If you drink a lot of caffeine containing beverages and you feel great, don't worry about it. If you're not feeling great, consider cutting down.

Caffeine can certainly interfere with sleep and folks who are sensitive to this effect may need to set a limit at one cup of coffee–before noon. Others may find even one cup too much. Anyone with high blood pressure, heart rhythm disturbances, anxiety, nervousness, irritability, or insomnia should probably reduce caffeine gradually and then eliminate caffeine completely for a few weeks to see if it helps. Individuals vary widely in their sensitivity to caffeine. The only sensible solution is to do what makes you feel healthier.

| KEEP UP WITH CALCIUM |

Everyone needs calcium to maintain healthy bones, but if you're female, fair skinned, thin, or petite you may need even more than most. Osteoporosis (literally porous bones) is a devastating condition that can turn old age into a nightmare. Bones weakened by calcium loss can become so fragile they break spontaneously. Loss of height, deformity from a humped back, and constant pain are the tragic results. Osteoporosis is less common in black women, (and men of any race.) But even folks with some degree of natural protection need a stable intake of calcium.

Dairy products are an excellent source of calcium, but they can't do the job all alone. Women generally require 1200 to 1500 mg of calcium per day. It's almost impossible to get that much calcium in a normal diet, so supplements are a good idea. Most calcium tablets come in 250 or 500 mg sizes and your best choice is one that contains magnesium as well.

One more word to the women at risk: calcium supplements alone cannot protect you against the ravages of osteoporosis. Weight bearing exercise (including swimming) is essential and estrogen replacement after menopause is controversial now. Don't try to handle this one on your own. Fighting osteoporosis is simply too important not to enlist the help of a physician.

| BRING ON BREAKFAST |

As a college student, I thought it odd that hardly anyone else ate breakfast. They were all dieting—unsuccessfully.

Interestingly, the people who stay trim throughout life are usually breakfast devotees. Some pack away a good-sized meal; others are content with a bowl of cereal or a piece of toast. But some sort of morning meal (besides a cream–filled donut at your coffee break) is important for maintaining productivity.

More than one study has shown that school children are more attentive and get better grades when they eat breakfast every morning. Adults are no different. Dragging through the morning gulping coffee or diet sodas is a decidedly bad idea. Instead recommend that your patients get up 20 minutes early and have a decent breakfast for three weeks. If they're not amazed at how much better they feel and how much more productive they are, they can always go back to their old ways. The increased energy level that comes from having breakfast may help those who are overweight lose a few pounds. Breakfast, anyone?

> SOME SORT OF MORNING MEAL...IS IMPORTANT FOR MAINTAINING PRODUCTIVITY.

| HELP YOURSELF TO WHOLE GRAINS |

There's nothing glamorous about eating whole grains but it can certainly improve your nutrition and gastrointestinal function. And those are two good ways of preserving a healthy body into old age. Whole grain cereals, breads, and rice should be part of almost everyone's diet. They're an excellent source of vitamins and fiber. (I suppose I had to use that word somewhere in this book.) I'm not recommending oat bran overload. No one food works magic when it comes to health. But a generous sprinkling of whole grains is a sensible addition to a healthy diet.

| FEAST ON FRESH FRUITS AND VEGETABLES |

If your patients already love fresh fruits and vegetables, they don't need any extra encouragement. But for many people, ketchup counts as a vegetable. Emphasize the role of fruits and vegetables in protecting them from chronic disease. Fresh fruits and vegetables are excellent sources of vitamins, minerals, and fiber. The beta–carotenes they contain help prevent some types of cancer. On top of that there are at least a few that can tempt anyone's taste buds. Brussels sprouts need not be your patients' first choice. Cherries and grapes and corn on the cob count. Even I can eat them.

| MINIMIZE MEAT |

Successful agers are generally not big meat eaters. They're not necessarily vegetarians but they do tend to have diets low in animal fats. Fortunately, much of the red meat produced today is lower in fat than was meat produced seven or eight years ago. Lean beef is an excellent source of protein, iron, and vitamin B_{12}. Limiting your intake of red meat to 4–6 ounces twice a week is a reasonable goal compatible with both good taste and long life.

| Dish Out the Fish |

Fish is a superior source of protein and omega–3 fatty acids (to keep your heart and brain happy) and, prepared properly, it's low in calories. Deep–fried shrimp and lobster dripping with butter are not in the running here. But fresh seafood can be scrumptious poached, baked, or broiled. It's a great way to keep the heart healthy and maintain a trim figure. Concern about mercury can be minimized by eating a wide variety of cold water fish caught in different coastal waters.

| Forego the Fats and Oils |

I've often joked about my four favorite food groups—flour, sugar, grease, and chocolate. But a high fat diet can lead to heart disease, gall bladder problems, and a variety of cancers. Aging successfully isn't an issue if you can't even make it past 60.

The real culprits are solid fats (lard, margarine) and tropical oils (palm, palm kernel, and coconut). If you must cook with oil, the best choices are corn oil, sunflower, canola seed, and olive oil, which is the best of all. Try to avoid store bought pastries, processed foods, and anything that's fried. Dairy products can be a double–edged sword because they're terrific sources of protein and calcium but the fat content can be deadly. Stick with skim or 1%, low fat (soft) cheese and yogurt. If your patients tasted the low fat stuff years ago and proclaimed it yucky, urge them to try again. Most of it tastes much better now. Folks demanded it.

| SHARE THE SWEETS |

I would be the world's biggest hypocrite if I suggested people give up sweets. A single perfect Belgian truffle approaches my idea of heaven. I believe everyone deserves a special treat now and then, which raises the issue of quality versus quantity. Savoring a single truffle does no harm to your health and can do wonders for your state of mind. But living on Twinkies and yo–yos is a good way to sabotage looks and health.

Once again, the key is moderation. But advise your patients that they don't need to stay entirely away from sweets. If they're at a fancy restaurant, and the dessert cart looks like a food fantasy, they needn't torment themselves. A better choice is to pick the desert they lust after and share it with an accomplice. It's satisfying and sensible. That's a tough combination to beat!

| SAVE YOUR SKIN |

There are three physical attributes that most people associate with the aging process: weight gain, gray hair, and wrinkles. An active lifestyle coupled with a balanced diet can ensure a trim figure. A good hairdresser can make the most of gray hair or cover it completely. But the ravages of sun exposure cannot be hidden so easily. They must be prevented if you want to look youthful longer. Ideally, sunscreen should be an integral part of our existence from early childhood on. Unfortunately, many of us have been around a lot longer than sunscreens. But, better late than never when it comes to saving your skin. Today, many brands of make-up and

> SUNSCREEN SHOULD BE AN INTEGRAL PART OF OUR EXISTENCE FROM EARLY CHILDHOOD ON.

moisturizers contain sunscreen. Sunscreen should be worn every day even when outdoor exposure is limited to as little as 10–15 minutes. Every little bit helps in the battle against premature aging and skin cancer.

| PREVENT THE PREVENTABLE |

Very few normal people like going to the doctor or dentist. Most of us do a superb job of putting off routine health care. It's time-consuming, it's boring, it's uncomfortable, and it's expensive. It's also the only way of preventing little problems from turning into big ones, which are even more time-consuming, uncomfortable, and expensive. Preventing the preventable is really not that difficult.

QUICK TIP FROM DR. O

USE THE FOLLOWING HEALTH CARE GUIDELINES AS A MEDICAL CHECKLIST FOR YOUR PATIENTS WHO WANT TO AGE SUCCESSFULLY.

* **TETANUS BOOSTER EVERY 10 YEARS.**

* **PNEUMONIA VACCINE FOR ANYONE OVER 60 OR PEOPLE WITH HEART DISEASE, LUNG PROBLEMS, OR DIABETES. REPEAT ABOUT EVERY 6 YEARS AFTER AGE 70.**

* **FLU SHOT EVERY YEAR FOR PEOPLE OVER 60.**

* **BLOOD PRESSURE CHECK EVERY 6 – 12 MONTHS.**

* **EYE EXAM EVERY 1–2 YEARS.**

* **HEARING CHECK EVERY 2–3 YEARS.**

* **PAP SMEAR EVERY YEAR FOR WOMEN UNTIL AGE 55, THEN EVERY 2 YEARS. MAMMOGRAMS EVERY YEAR FOR WOMEN OVER 50.**

* **RECTAL EXAM FOR MEN AND WOMEN EVERY YEAR OVER 40.**

* **CHOLESTEROL PROFILE AS A BASELINE AND AS RECOMMENDED BY YOUR DOCTOR.**

* **BLOOD TESTS, URINALYSIS, CHEST X-RAY, AND EKG AS RECOMMENDED BY A PHYSICIAN.**

* **PERIODIC BLOOD SUGAR LEVELS AND THYROID FUNCTION STUDIES.**

CHAPTER 4

SAFEGUARDING YOURSELF AGAINST SERIOUS STRESS

Extreme remedies are very often appropriate for extreme diseases.

—*Hippocrates*

Medical researchers and physicians are often hesitant to proclaim stress a risk factor for serious illness. The reason is simple. Stress is, at least, so far, impossible to quantify. We can attach a number to cholesterol or blood sugar or blood pressure or a host of other parameters of health. But we can't pin a number on stress. Research into the effects of stress could proceed much faster if we could say, "Aha! A serum stress level of 274 mg per deciliter." Perhaps someday we'll learn how to measure things like stress, pain, and anxiety in an objective way. But for now we can only rely on our perceptions.

It's no surprise that preventing serious stress is preferable to struggling with it after the fact. Unfortunately, stress has a nasty way of sneaking up on its victims. People often have a remarkable ability to cope with a stressful situation that's isolated and well defined. The adrenal glands kick in, you do what needs to be done and then once the problem is resolved, you relax. During the crisis and war in the Persian Gulf, many service members and families found the actual war less stressful than the preceding waiting and uncertainty. Not that any phase of such a crisis is simple or easy, but the human nervous system is geared toward action and resolution. It's not well equipped for long periods of tense uncertainty.

> **PROLONGED, UNRESOLVED STRESS IS INCOMPATIBLE WITH SUCCESSFUL AGING.**

Prolonged, unresolved stress is incompatible with successful aging. No one can eliminate stress completely, but we can learn to prevent much of it and deal with the rest constructively. The "secrets" that follow can help your patients safeguard themselves against the serious, insidious stress that undermines health and happiness.

| SET ASIDE A SAFETY VALVE |

Our minds need relaxation, and give way!
Unless we mix with work a little play.
– Moliere

Moliere knew what he was talking about. Learning how to relax is essential in the battle against stress. It sounds so easy, and yet millions of people find it nearly impossible to unwind and relax completely. Some people are convinced they simply don't have the time (which is probably the most important time to relax). But even having abundant leisure time does not guarantee the ability to truly relax. It's possible to have nothing to do and still be a nervous wreck.

Relaxation is a profoundly personal issue. Jogging five miles may accomplish for one person a degree of relaxation available to another only through deep meditation. The key is determining what works best for you and then doing it on a regular basis. It's difficult to imagine anyone busier than the president. And yet, he and most of his predecessors have formally incorporated relaxing activities into their hectic schedules. There's nothing self–indulgent about it. In fact, regular relaxation is an essential part of sustaining first rate performance on the job.

If you're serious about getting a handle on stress, stop and think of the five most relaxing activities you enjoy. When was the last time you did any of them? If it has been more than a few days, you need to remedy the situation. Walk, swim, golf, sit in the sauna or simply sleep, but do something relaxing every day. It's the best safety valve for serious stress.

| SLUMBER SOUNDLY |

Oh sleep! It is a gentle thing! Beloved from pole to pole!
–Samuel Taylor Coleridge

The ability to sleep soundly is often an excellent indicator of good mental and physical health. Of course, almost everyone has a restless night now and then. Situational anxiety, stress, illness, or grief can wreak havoc with restful sleep. Problems arise when insufficient, excessive, or poor quality sleep becomes routine.

Unfortunately, insomnia and other sleep disturbances tend to feed on themselves. A few sleepless nights can lead to daytime fatigue, lethargy and somnolence, which further disrupt the normal sleep–wake cycle. Nervousness, anxiety, irritability, and difficulty concentrating can make the daylight hours seem like a nightmare.

The aging process often leaves its own mark on one's ability to sleep. Generally, as people grow older they require less sleep and spend less time in the deepest levels of sleep. Frustration mounts when early bedtimes or daytime naps result in long periods of staring at the clock in the middle of the night.

> INSOMNIA CAN RESULT IN DEPRESSION, MEMORY PROBLEMS, FALLS AND LOWER QUALITY OF LIFE IN OLDER ADULTS.

A recent study published in Geriatrics in 2004 noted that sleep problems occur in over half of adults over age 65, not because of age but rather the comorbidities that come with the passing years. Insomnia can result in depression, memory problems, falls and lower quality of life in older adults. Lack of restful sleep can even lead to adverse changes in the way the body functions, according to the researchers.

Fortunately, it is possible to retrain oneself and develop good sleep habits.

If some of your patients can't remember their last good night's sleep, recommend trying the following "secrets" for three weeks. It takes that long to develop a new habit, but the results are well worth the effort.

| SECRETS OF SOUND SLEEP |

1. Get up and go to bed at the same time every day.
2. Use the bedroom only for sleeping or lovemaking. Eat, write, read, or watch TV elsewhere.
3. Keep the bedroom cool, dark, quiet, and clean.
4. Exercise enough to get physically tired every day but avoid exertion after dinner.
5. Keep caffeine to a minimum and have it before noon.

6.   Avoid alcohol and nicotine.

7.   Eliminate daytime naps.

8.   Establish a bedtime routine (e.g. hot bath, skin care, selecting tomorrow's clothes, etc.)

9.   Relax with a period of quiet time, soft music, reading before going to bed.

10.   Keep a clear conscience.

11.   If you can't sleep, don't stay in bed. Get up and read or putter around the house.

12.   Force yourself to stay up until you're really sleepy. Don't go to bed at 8:00PM just because you're bored.

13.   Don't eat tomato products, greasy snacks or spicy foods if they give you heartburn. Heartburn gets worse when you lie down, and can make falling asleep difficult. The discomfort of heartburn can also awaken some people in the middle of the night.

14.   Restrict fluids before bedtime to limit awakenings during the night to urinate.

15. If noise is disturbing your sleep (say, the rumble of passing trains or a partner's snoring) consider earplugs, rugs or drapes to muffle sound, or relaxing music or tapes.

16. Make sure your mattress is comfortable or supportive. Some good ways to know you need a new mattress: You wake up with your back aching or you sleep better when you're away from home.

It's a good idea to ask your elderly patients about the quality of their sleep. Good health is impossible without good sleep. A variety of conditions including heart disease, lung disease, diabetes, hyperthyroidism, hot flashes and prostate problems can impair sound sleep. Thus sleep problems may be an important indicator of underlying morbidity.

| WORK UP A SWEAT |

It is better to wear out than to rust out.
–Richard Cumberland

Exercise is essential for good health and weight control but it's also a marvelous way to combat stress. This is no surprise to athletes who, when unable to exercise, can become downright grouchy. However, many people with a busy but sedentary lifestyle overlook this extraordinary natural tranquilizer.

Particularly busy people often voice the greatest resistance to exercise, as did this 38–year–old bank

> **LACK OF TIME AND ENERGY IS THE MOST COMMON EXCUSE FOR NOT EXERCISING.**

vice president and mother of two, "My whole life is a rat race! I'm up at 5, get the kids dressed and fed, drop them off at school and day care, race around to meetings and conferences for 8 or 10 or 12 hours, cook dinner, clean the house and collapse. I don't have time for exercise." She's not alone.

Lack of time and energy is the most common excuse for not exercising. And yet, the great paradox of exercise is that it actually boosts energy, stamina, and efficiency. Reading that statement will not convince an unbeliever. You have to actually feel the tremendous difference that working up a good sweat can make.

Quick Tip From Dr. O

IF ONE OF YOUR PATIENTS IS LAUNCHING A NEW WORKOUT PROGRAM, PROVIDE HIM OR HER WITH A FEW SENSIBLE TIPS:

* **CHOOSE AN ACTIVITY YOU FIND PLEASANT AND FEASIBLE.**

* **START OUR SLOWLY AND BUILD UP GRADUALLY IF YOU HAVE ANY UNDERLYING HEALTH PROBLEMS.**

* **IF YOU'RE OVER 45, ASK A HEALTH PROFESSIONAL WHICH EXERCISE IS POSSIBLE, AND WHAT ACTIVITY MAY BE A GOOD MATCH FOR YOU.**

* **COMMIT YOURSELF TO BEING ACTIVE FOR LIFE.**

* **HAVE FUN WITH IT.**

Exercise keeps you trim, bolsters the immune system, strengthen the heart, improves sleep, boosts energy, and relieves stress. No pill on the planet can do all that!

| INSIST ON QUIET TIME |

The best thinking has been done in solitude.
The worst has been done in turmoil
—Thomas Alva Edison

Noise pollution is a cardinal enemy of successful aging. The constant roar of motors and engines and machines can harm the psyche as well as the inner ear. But an equally dangerous and far more insidious form of noise pollution is found inside virtually every American home – TV, often accompanied by radios, VCRs, DVDs and video games.

It's a rare home that isn't plagued by such sounds 18 hours a day. And this is a relatively new phenomenon. Seventy or 80 years ago, people enjoyed a much quieter life. The still of the night was broken only by the sounds of music or conversation. Today "the still of the night" is little more than a quaint cliché.

Successful agers know the value of quiet time. A 96-year-old lady with the face, body, and mind of someone 30 years younger described its therapeutic effects, "I haven't had an easy life but it's been a fine one just the same. My mother taught me that I could cope with anything as long as I set aside 30 minutes morning and night of total silence. Now that's harder than it sounds when you've got a husband and children to contend with, but I did it and, by golly, it worked. It still does."

The importance of quiet time is not a new concept. It's downright ancient. Monks and mystics and philosophers throughout the ages have placed great value on solitude and silence. Jesus made a point of getting away from it all periodically, as did Mohammed and Buddha. Quiet time does wonders for a person's soul and psyche. And, it's not bad for the body, either.

Like exercise, regularly scheduled quiet time will reduce stress levels and boost energy. In fact, the more frazzled your patients are, the more it will help. Even 20 minutes of complete quiet twice a day can work wonders.

> QUIET TIME DOES WONDERS FOR A PERSON'S SOUL AND PSYCHE

| CONSULT A CONFIDANTE |

Friendship multiplies the good of life and divides the evil.
'Tis the sole remedy against misfortune, the very ventilation of the soul.
—Baltasar Gracian

The people who truly age successfully are not lonely and isolated. They nurture close, loving relationships regardless of their marital state. But no matter how big their family or circle of friends, successful agers know they can rely on at least one close confidante.

No one gets through life without a few serious problems. But sharing those problems with a trustworthy, nonjudgmental confidante can alleviate tremendous stress and often expedite solutions. This is not the same as whining about each annoyance to every acquaintance in sight. The key to maintaining a close confidante is reciprocity. You must be there for each other as Betty, a bright 86 year old explains:

> *Martha and I have been best friends for*
> *66 years. We've seen each other through*

weddings, births, miscarriages, illnesses, wars, and the deaths of our husbands.

She knows me better than anyone in the world. Sharing a cup of tea with Martha is the best therapy I know. Too bad young people today don't know that kind of friendship.

Nurturing that kind of friendship takes time and commitment, two things most people find difficult to juggle in our frantic, fast-paced society. But making time for friendship can improve the present and pave the way for a happy future. It's one of the best investments we can make for old age.

| PAMPER YOURSELF |

Gather ye rosebuds while ye may, / Old Time is still a-flying! And This same flower that smiles to-day / Tomorrow will be dying.
—Robert Herrick

Pampering yourself may sound self-indulgent, narcissistic, or at least undisciplined. It's certainly not the way most of us were raised. And yet, it's a superb way to prevent or combat serious stress. Pampering oneself is one of the truly fun secrets of successful aging. And it's can benefit both stressed–out health professionals and their patients.

What makes for effective pampering is different for everyone. Some type A personalities can't stand the thought of staying in bed long enough to eat breakfast. For others, breakfast in bed approaches nirvana.

In today's world, millions of people struggling to cope with careers, families, and scores of other commitments feel guilty about enjoying themselves. Enjoying life is good. It's what we're supposed to do.

Sadly enough some people get into such a rut that they can't think of ways to pamper themselves. Women have a particular problem with this, especially if they have children or aging parents to care for. If you don't know precisely what it takes to feel pampered, consider the following list. If you see something intriguing, give it a try. You might stumble upon a great way to beat stress.

| WAYS TO FEEL PAMPERED |

1. Take a bubble bath.

2. Wear your favorite perfume for no reason.

3. Have dinner by candlelight.

4. Do anything by candlelight.

5. Take a long walk.

6. Have a professional manicure.

7. Savor your very favorite food.

8. Get a massage.

9. Turn off the phone and listen to your favorite music.

10. Make a date for a 2–hour lunch.

11. Relax in a sauna or hot tub.

12. Have a professional facial.

13. Wear your most beautiful nightgown for yourself.

14. Declare an hour of silence.

15. Spend a whole day in your bathrobe.

16. Sip champagne with a friend just because.

17. Take a weekend mini–vacation.

18. Read old love letters.

19. Make popcorn and watch an old movie.

20. Have a weekly "beauty" night.

The possibilities are virtually endless. What matters is doing something really special for yourself on a regular basis. What can be even nicer is finding a partner and doing something special for each other. But remember, if you can't be good to yourself it's very difficult to be good to someone else. Successful agers are good to those around them but they start by being good to themselves.

| ASK FOR ASSISTANCE |

Independence? That's middle class blasphemy. We are all dependent on one another, every soul of us on earth.
—George Bernard Shaw

We all experience periods of greater and lesser stress in our lives. All too often, the periods of greater stress correspond with our mistaken belief that we must manage everything all alone. How many women convince themselves that no one else could possibly do the shopping, cook the meals, watch the kids, clean the house, close the new deal at the office, or run the church fundraiser? People are always willing to let some self–proclaimed dynamo do all the work. And yet, when that dynamo is suddenly out of commission by virtue of accident, illness, or death, the essential things still get done.

The trick is to ask for assistance before disaster strikes. Most husbands and children are perfectly capable of helping more than they do. Friends and colleagues can pitch in and help one another. And finally, help with almost any project can be purchased.

> ENDING UP IN A HOSPITAL WITH SOME STRESS RELATED ILLNESS IS A FAR GREATER WASTE OF MONEY.

That's right. Purchased. This is a stumbling block for lots of compulsive, thrifty people. Even people with hefty incomes convince themselves that paying someone to clean the house, wash the windows, mow the yard, or care for children is wasteful or extravagant. I like to point out that ending up in a hospital with some stress related illness is a far greater waste of money. Nancy, a 34 year old mother of three and part–time teacher, resisted the idea of paying someone to help with housework. The family income of $42,000 was too tight for such an extravagance, or so she thought.

I was exhausted all the time, frazzled, and irritable. But I balked when my husband suggested we get help. It seemed so indulgent and expensive. Well, eventually I gave it a try out of sheer exhaustion. We arranged to pay someone $50 to help with the heavier chores every other week. I couldn't believe the difference it made. We adjusted our budget and now I get a clean house and some semblance of sanity for $100 a month. It's certainly better than spending $100 a month for antidepressants.

Asking for assistance is a wise choice. Pay for it, if you must. But don't let chronic exhaustion rule your life or your patients' lives. It's a one—way ticket to premature aging.

| PLAY. |

It is a happy talent to know how to play.
—Emerson

No one is ever too old to play and yet, in our high pressure, chaotic culture the art of play is often lost shortly after college if not before. Playing seems so childish and unproductive. And it is, which is exactly why it's an essential ingredient in successful aging.

The best commentary on play I've heard came from Max, a 101—year—old farmer, "I always worked mighty hard, long hours and lots of sweat. But I played hard, too. Still do, for that matter. I can teach my great—great grandchildren a thing or two about havin' fun. Work hard, play hard, be good to folks and have fun doin' all of it. I reckon that's what life's all about." There's little more I can add to that except for a few suggestions as a jump—start:

1. Take a little kid to the zoo.

2. Adopt a kitten.

3. Eat an ice cream cone – with jimmies.

4. Ride a merry–go–round.

5. Watch "Fantasia", "The Little Mermaid" or "Lady and the Tramp".

6. Build a sandcastle.

7. Have a pillow fight.

8. Catch snowflakes on your tongue.

9. Make hot chocolate and watch cartoons.

10. Catch lightning bugs.

11. Go to a costume party or have one.

12. Celebrate Christmas in July.

13. Watch clouds.

14. Pick daisies.

15. Sing out loud.

16. Dance.

17. Have a picnic.

18. Go on a treasure hunt.

19. Read a Dr. Suess book.

20. Pretend anything.

| SAFEGUARDING YOURSELF AGAINST SERIOUS STRESS |

5 MAKING THE MOST OF YOUR MIND AND MEMORY

I do not believe that the same God who has endowed us with sense, reason, and intellect has intended us to forego their use.
—Galileo Galilei

People share many fears about growing old, but perhaps the greatest is the fear of losing one's mind and memory. Indeed the sight of a poor demented Alzheimer's victim unable to recognize spouse or children leaves us all devastated. Without a clear mind and sound memory, longevity loses much, if not all, of its appeal. Who would want to reach 80, 90, or 100 years deprived of a clear mind and a lifetime of memories?

Unfortunately, the scientific community and public alike have long assumed that cognitive decline and memory loss were an inherent part of the aging process. And yet, there have always been intellectual and artistic giants conquering new horizons despite their advanced years. Grandma Moses, Pablo Casals, Irving Berlin, Helen Hayes, and a host of others defied the myth that old age equals mental demise.

Are such geriatric wonders simply the beneficiaries of good genes or good luck? They may have had their share of both but a far more likely explanation lies in their incessant striving for improvement—a better painting, a richer tone, a lovelier melody, and a more captivating performance. Successful agers never retire from self-improvement and intellectual challenge. They exercise their minds every bit as much as their bodies.

If you learn and challenge yourself throughout life, your brain will grow. Literally. An active, lively brain constructs new dendrites, or synaptic connections between neurons that help brain cells communicate. The result is that the brain can store and retrieve information with greater ease.

> SUCCESSFUL AGERS NEVER RETIRE FROM SELF-IMPROVEMENT AND INTELLECTUAL CHALLENGE.

Unused muscles quickly atrophy. So does an unused mind. Although modern medicine has much to learn about the aging brain, there are ways to maximize your brain power and reduce the likelihood of cognitive decline. Making the most of your mind and memory is much like physical exercise – it only works when done on a regular basis.

| NEVER STOP LEARNING |

Anyone who stops learning is old, whether at 20 or 80. Anyone who keeps learning stays young. The greatest thing in life is to keep your mind young.
–Henry Ford

The thought that formal education ends upon graduation from high school, college, or professional school is quite common in our culture. It's also preposterous. If you're not learning something new every day of your life, you're frittering away your very existence.

For decades, if not centuries, prevailing wisdom has held that learning ability declines with age. But presuming normal intelligence, learning is largely dependent on motivation and practice. If a 70-year-old person hasn't bothered to learn anything new in 40 years, the culprits are likely to be disinterest and lack of practice, not a certain number of birthdays.

Though the pace of learning changes as one grows older, fears of age-related mental decline are often exaggerated. Three key factors result in good mental function in one's elder years: regular exercise, an extended social support system, and one's ability to cope with what life has to offer.

Given genuine interest and regular practice, older individuals can learn every bit as well as their younger colleagues. So don't waste another minute. Make a solemn vow to learn something new every day. Then do it!

| KEEP UP WITH CURRENT EVENTS |

The education of man is never completed until he dies.
–Robert E. Lee

One of the saddest stereotypes of old age is the tendency to live in the past. Not that fond memories aren't wonderful or a little nostalgia touching, but living in a time warp is unproductive. It's also painfully dull. The real movers and shakers of any generation are far too busy with present activities and future plans to wallow in yesteryear.

Keeping abreast of current events involves more than watching the evening news, however. News is important, but as you may have noticed, it tends to be negative. The goal here is not to engender a major clinical depression. Senior citizens need to stay informed, not infuriated.

Those who are at retirement age can take the time to read about the "why" behind the headlines. They'll gain

> ONE OF THE SADDEST STEREOTYPES OF OLD AGE IS THE TENDENCY TO LIVE IN THE PAST.

tremendous insight into the historic, geographic, economic, political, cultural, and philosophical forces that shape our world. The insights gained may spur elders to take up a worthy cause or tackle a new challenge.

It's also important for seniors to keep up with current trends in music, art, literature, and fashion. Every piece of music written after 1958 is not "garbage." One of the most reliable markers of a "sour old poop" is the staunch conviction that the only decent music is the kind popular when "I was a teenager." Even the waltz was an outrage at one time!

| READ, READ, READ |

The man who does not read good books has no
advantage over the man who cannot read them.
—Mark Twain

Have you ever noticed that people who love to read are usually successful? They also tend to be interesting and appealing. People who read want something more out of life, something better than the status quo. That makes them winners. The losers of the world don't care about self-development. They don't read. And it shows.

> PEOPLE WHO READ WANT SOMETHING MORE OUT OF LIFE, SOMETHING BETTER THAN THE STATUS QUO.

As a geriatrician, I'm constantly approached by people wondering if there is a way to prevent Alzheimer's disease or dementia. The standard advice includes controlling blood pressure to prevent strokes, eating a low fat diet to prevent arteriosclerosis, limiting alcohol, avoiding cigarettes, staying active, etc. But I've noticed over the years that avid readers develop dementing illnesses less often than others do, and when they do, their decline seems less rapid.

Others have observed this phenomenon but it hasn't been proven yet by vigorous scientific methods. On a purely intuitive level the concept has some merit: the more knowledge and wisdom and skill you have, the longer it takes to deteriorate. I suspect the validity of this theory will be clinically and scientifically proven in the next few years. But why wait? Reading is like aerobic exercise for the brain. Use it or lose it.

| EXPAND YOUR FRAME OF REFERENCE |

Minds, like bodies, will often fall into a pimpled,
ill-conditioned state from mere excess of comfort.
— Charles Dickens

Everyone agrees there's a first time for everything. But as the years go by, it's easy to get in a rut. The problem is deadly. The rut becomes a groove and the groove becomes a grave.

I must admit I never really thought much about expanding one's frame of reference as a secret of successful aging. That is, until I met a 68-year-old novice skydiver. She (that's right, she) explained it this way:

> *"I always led a normal, predictable life. High school, secretarial job, marriage, children, retirement. I was content, until widowhood hit me like a bolt of lightning. Suddenly my life had the appeal of a dish towel. Everything about me seemed so horribly ordinary. I couldn't stand the thought of being like every other 68-year-old widow in the world. I was obsessed with the need to be different. I wanted adventure, challenge, and excitement. When I saw a clip of the Golden Knights parachute team a few weeks later, the bug hit me! The thought of danger never crossed my mind. I wanted that feeling of exhilaration!"*

| CHAPTER 5 |

Well, she got it. After beginning a graduated exercise program, this 68-year-old would-be daredevil began skydiving lessons. She loves every minute of it. Half of her friends and family think she's nuts and the other half wish they had the nerve to join her. I'm not recommending skydiving as an antidote to old age. But if something gets you this fired up–go for it. But be warned-this sort of endeavor can lead to intoxicating levels of fun!

| TURN OFF THE TV |

The majority of people waste virtually every evening & weekend on trivia.
–Dr. Walter Doyle Staples

If the mere thought of losing your mind or memory strikes terror into the core of your being, for heaven's sake, turn the TV off! I'm being slightly melodramatic, but only slightly. More than a few studies have shown that people who watch more than four hours of TV each day are apt to be bored, irritable, depressed and restless. They also have problems sleeping, concentrating, and remembering things. TV can be a godsend to people in a hospital or nursing home. And, there are some excellent educational and cultural programs. But if you're sacked out in front of the television for more than two or three hours a day—max—you need a life!

| ACTIVATE YOUR BODY |

Exercise can preserve something of our early strength even into old age.
—Cicero

What does physical exercise have to do with your mind and memory? Plenty. Older men who exercised on a regular basis for two years scored higher on tests of memory and cognitive function. The connection between mind and body is inescapable. Anything you do to improve your cardio-pulmonary function will enhance circulation-including circulation to your brain. Exercise also reduces secretion of the body's stress hormones and promotes release of endorphins—the brain's own natural "feel good" chemicals.

THE CONNECTION BETWEEN MIND AND BODY IS INESCAPABLE.

Now you have even more good reasons to exercise. If you forgot the others, go back to Chapter III and re-read the section on Learning to Like Exercise. Then get out there and do it!

| CONTROL YOUR BLOOD PRESSURE |

A man is as old as his arteries.
–Henry Cazalis

Most people know that high blood pressure does bad things to your body—heart disease, strokes, and kidney damage to name a few. But did you know that uncontrolled high blood pressure can cause the second most common form of dementia? Unfortunately, it does.

Vascular dementia is the result of many small strokes that often go unrecognized. Tiny strokes in areas of the brain that don't result in paralysis or trouble speaking take a serious toll, nonetheless. Typically, people will develop a stepwise, episodic decline in mental function, memory, judgment, and functional ability. Diabetes is often a contributing factor, but high blood pressure can do it alone. Making the most of one's mind and memory often means having blood pressure checked every 4 to 6 months. The best way to treat vascular dementia is to prevent it!

| Take the Right Supplements |

If I'd known I was going to live so long, I'd have taken better care of myself
—Leon Eldred

Are there respectable quantities of fresh fruit and vegetables in your diet? Do you take extra Vitamin C & E every day? Would you be willing to start if you knew those practices might reduce your chances of developing Alzheimer's? What would you advise your patients about taking supplements?

Growing research evidence is indicating that some vitamins and antioxidants do protect against dementia. Folks who have a lifetime pattern of consuming more antioxidants, seem more likely to escape the ravages of Alzheimer's disease.

But, wait. There's more. Recently, we've discovered that people who take anti-inflammatory drugs like ibuprofen, or naprosyn are less likely to develop Alzheimer's. Is it wise to advise your patients to start scarfing down handfuls of Motrin, Aleve, or Vitamin E? Hardly. But eating plenty of fresh fruits and vegetables, taking sensible vitamin supplements (250 mg Vitamin C twice a day and 100 to 400 International units of Vitamin E every day) is a good idea. As for the naproxen and ibuprofen? Well, researchers are working to discover the true protective effect of these medicines.

| ABSTAIN FROM ALCOHOL |

Long quaffing maketh a short life.
–John Lyly

We talked about this one in Chapter III. Alcohol is directly toxic to the brain. Every time you drink enough to feel good, you've probably knocked off a few thousand brain cells. Do this over a lifetime and you won't be pleased with what's left. Alcohol dementia syndrome is a devastating problem that's far from rare. You don't need to be a falling-down drunk to develop it. Can alcohol relax you? Yes. Can it reduce the likelihood of developing coronary artery disease? Possibly. Are you willing to risk what this can do to your mind and memory? I'm not. No

> ALCOHOL IS DIRECTLY TOXIC TO THE BRAIN.

need to become a fanatic, just keep it on the light side. Going

light on alcohol often results in being sharp as a tack at 90.

> THE REAL MASTERS OF SUCCESSFUL
> AGING CONSTANTLY HAVE A FRESH
> CHALLENGE BEFORE THEM.

| CHASE A NEW CHALLENGE |

When I was young, I was amazed at Plutarch's statement
that the elder Cato began at the age of 80 to learn Greek. I
am amazed no longer. Old age is ready to undertake tasks
that youth shirked because they would take too long.
—W. Somerset Maugham

Quick! What was the last thing you did that really stretched

your abilities to the max? How long ago was it? If it was any time

in the past month, congratulations! Double congratulations

if you're over 60. If it was over a year ago, you need to get

on the stick.

The real masters of successful aging constantly have

a fresh challenge before them. And they're often quick to

emphasize that they don't cope with problems, they tackle

challenges. Silly semantics? Not on your life. Attitude is everything, especially as we age.

❀ QUICK TIP FROM DR. O

BRACE YOURSELF, AND CONSIDER THIS:

* ANNA MARY (GRANDMA) MOSES BEGAN HER PAINTING CAREER AT AGE 76 WHEN ARTHRITIS MADE IT TOO PAINFUL TO DO NEEDLEWORK ANY LONGER.

* MARIAN HART FLEW A SINGLE ENGINE PLANE IN A SOLO TRANSATLANTIC FLIGHT IN 1975. SHE WAS 84.

* FRANK LLOYD WRIGHT BEGAN HIS MOST CREATIVE WORK AT AGE 69. THE GUGGENHEIM MUSEUM IN NEW YORK WAS COMPLETED WHEN HE WAS 91.

* BERTRAND RUSSELL, BRITISH PHILOSOPHER, FORMED A NUCLEAR DISARMAMENT GROUP AT AGE 88. AT AGE 90 HE INTERVENED WITH HEADS OF STATE DURING THE CUBAN MISSILE CRISIS.

* ALBERT SCHWEITZER CARED FOR PATIENTS AT HIS HOSPITAL IN LAMBARENE, GABON FROM AGE 84 TO 90.

Now what was that about being too old?

| MAKE THE MOST OF MUSIC |

There is nothing more remarkable in the life of Socrates
than that he found time in his old age to learn to dance
and play on instruments and thought it time well spent.
—Montaigne

Music and memory are intimately connected. But, at present, no one knows exactly how or why. Many studies have demonstrated enhanced learning ability and retention of material studied while soft, slow classical music played in the background. Folks who play a musical instrument actively develop their memories in a way non-musicians can't. Of course, most musicians learn their skill in childhood or adolescence. But there's no law of the universe preventing anyone from learning to play an instrument at any age. All we really need is interest and desire. Contrary to popular belief, talent represents a fairly small part of the equation. Anyone willing to practice diligently enough can learn to play a few tunes.

Music therapy is being used with increasingly good results in a variety of clinical or medical settings. The right music can boost energy, calm anger, quiet hyperactivity, relieve boredom, ease depression and fear, inspire strength and courage, promote relaxation, enhance prayer and meditation and foster clear thinking. Classical music is especially good for honing the mind.

If you've never been a classical music lover, you probably haven't heard enough of the "good stuff." It's not too late. There's a reason classical music is referred to as "high brow." If you really want to make the most of your mind and memory, make the most of classical music.

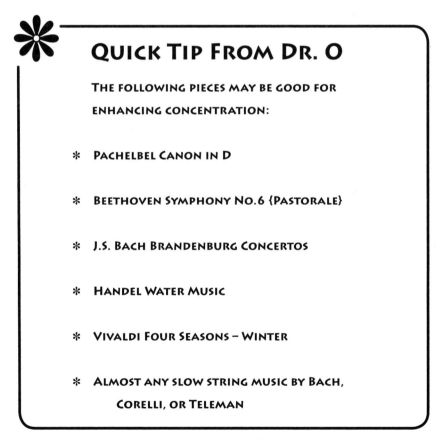

QUICK TIP FROM DR. O

THE FOLLOWING PIECES MAY BE GOOD FOR ENHANCING CONCENTRATION:

* **PACHELBEL CANON IN D**

* **BEETHOVEN SYMPHONY NO.6 {PASTORALE}**

* **J.S. BACH BRANDENBURG CONCERTOS**

* **HANDEL WATER MUSIC**

* **VIVALDI FOUR SEASONS – WINTER**

* **ALMOST ANY SLOW STRING MUSIC BY BACH, CORELLI, OR TELEMAN**

| SET GOALS - AND WRITE THEM DOWN |

Happiness is the progressive realization of a worthy goal.
—Emerson

Sadly, the vast majority of people haven't got a clue about what they want or where they're going in life. No wonder they're bored or depressed when they get there! The practice of setting clear, specific goals can have a greater impact on your life than almost any other piece of advice. It may well be the premiere secret of successful aging.

But this does not seem to be common knowledge! Most folks spend more time planning some silly party or 2 week vacation than they spend planning their life's purpose! Don't fall into this trap. As Benjamin Franklin said, "Dost thou love life? Then do not squander time, for that's the stuff life is made of." If you don't have clear, specific written goals it's extremely likely you're squandering big chunks of your life.

In 1953, a group of researchers studied members of the graduating class at Yale University. Only 3 percent had comprehensive written goals. No surprise there. The follow-up leg of the study done in 1973 revealed that the 3 percent with written goals had greater career achievements and overall life satisfaction than the others. But here's the real kicker: that 3 percent also had accumulated more wealth than the other 97 percent COMBINED! There is power in the written word.

QUICK TIP FROM DR. O

THREE GOOD BOOKS ON ATTAINING LIFE GOALS INCLUDE:

* **THINK AND GROW RICH**
  NAPOLEON HILL

* **THE MAGIC OF THINKING BIG**
  DAVID SCHWARTZ

* **THINK LIKE A WINNER**
  DR. WALTER DOYLE STAPLES

Your education, no matter how basic or lofty is incomplete until you've mastered the wonderful principles in these books. The art and science of setting goals will keep the mind, memory, soul and body younger than any pill or potion can.

CHAPTER 6
CELEBRATE YOUR SOCIAL LIFE

Have friends. 'Tis a second existence.

—*Baltasar Gracian*

One of the greatest tragedies of old age is the profound loneliness that afflicts so many people. Every day I see despondent elderly patients in the nursing home or hospital who ache for want of a single friend. Their pain is palpable.

Is this dreadful scenario simply part of the human condition, a price one pays for outliving others? The answer, according to many sagacious elders, is a resounding "no"! There are ways to guard against certain illnesses and injuries. There are strategies to prevent financial hardship and poverty. And there are behaviors that vastly reduce the chances of living in social isolation and abandonment.

If you've ever worried about facing your final years alone, you'll want to pay special attention to the secrets that follow. They come highly recommended by some very happy folks in their 80's and 90's, who have an abundance of love, friendship, and affection.

| LOOK FOR THE GOOD |

Goodness is the only investment that never fails.
—Thoreau

Remember when you first fell in love? Everything about your Prince or Princess Charming was wonderful. His eyes, his smile, his walk, his laugh were positively endearing. He was cute or smart or witty or dashing or all of the above. You couldn't wait to be with him, every moment apart was torture. Still feel that way?

Why not? Because you started noticing the bad, annoying habits, physical flaws, personal faults, various shortcomings. But, if you're honest, you probably didn't stop at taking mere notice. No. You probably began to dwell on them, focus on them, and nag about them. After a while it's difficult to remember what attracted you in the first place!

Love, friendship, passion and romance cannot survive in a negative environment. Have you ever known someone who practically emitted a force field of negativity? Nothing ever suited them, the weather was always awful, nobody else ever did anything right, they always felt terrible, and on and on and on. We all know the type—they brighten a room by leaving it. Is there a chance—however remote—that you've been this negative? Don't feel defensive, it can happen to anyone. In fact, in our society, it will happen unless you take daily steps to guard against it. All we have to do is turn on the TV or radio or pick up a newspaper and we're bombarded with negative stories and people.

> LOVE, FRIENDSHIP, PASSION AND ROMANCE CANNOT SURVIVE IN A NEGATIVE ENVIRONMENT.

The only solution is to launch a self-directed counter-attack. Bombard oneself with positive thoughts—uplifting books, inspiring music, educational tapes, constructive conversation. Associate with positive, successful people. Look for whatever is good in any situation or person. When you focus on the good you'll attract good people and good occurrences like a magnet.

| LET GO OF GRUDGES |

To be wronged is nothing unless you continue to remember it.
–Confucius

How can you spend the last 20 or 30 years of life alone and miserable? I have the answer. You can concentrate on some person who wronged you or treated you unkindly years ago. The situation only gets worse if you concentrate on that incident and blows it way out of proportion. The incident turns into one of the most significant events in human history. If people dwell on the ways they were wronged, anger, hostility, and resentment can consume them. They begin to wallow in bitterness. Now let me ask you-would you want to

GRUDGES ARE A LIFETIME PASS TO LONELINESS.

spend much time with a person who had poisoned himself this way?

No one else would, either. And yet, there's something almost seductive about the righteous indignation that holding a grudge generates. People seem to savor it, in a perverse sort of way. But grudges are a lifetime pass to loneliness. Often, the villain who wronged you probably forgot it years ago. He may even be dead. So, don't torment yourself over past injustices. As they say (in their collective wisdom), living well is the best revenge.

| DARE TO BE DIFFERENT |

I shall be telling this with a sigh. Somewhere ages and ages hence: Two roads diverged in a wood, and I – took the one less traveled by, And that has made all the difference.
–Robert Frost

Anyone out there really looking forward to being "another old retired guy?" How about a generic "little old lady?" Some may scoff, but the more highly you prize conformity, the more likely you'll be to merit those labels. The mere thought of such obscurity makes me shudder. I hope it stirs the same reaction in you.

| CELEBRATE YOUR SOCIAL LIFE |

Not that all of us don't appreciate people with whom we share common interests and experiences. That creates a sense of belonging, which is wonderful, indeed. But relentless predictability and conformity is boring. And boredom is one of the fastest routes to premature aging I know.

Of course, daring to be different requires healthy self-esteem. People will notice you. A few may laugh but most onlookers will secretly wish they had your guts or moxy or style. It doesn't matter if you're the only woman in church wearing a hat or the only man on the block too busy to watch the Super Bowl. Dare to be different.

| CAN THE CRITICISM |

People ask you for criticism, but they only want praise.
—William Somerset Maugham

Any turkey can criticize people. And they usually do. It has become a national pastime! How often do you pick up a newspaper or turn on the evening news and hear people offering practical solutions to any given problem? Hardly ever. What you hear is an endless barrage of criticism, much of it rendered in a nasty, condescending manner.

And what about the scene at work? Heard much positive, uplifting conversation during lunch or coffee breaks? Unlikely. But are things any better at home? How much criticism is bandied about at the kitchen table?

> **IT'S BEST TO REPLACE CRITICISM WITH KINDNESS.**

Don't feel too bad. It's human nature. Criticizing people, policies, or programs is a lot easier than changing them or yourself.

But constructive criticism can be helpful, you say. Well, I'm not so sure. Many people have been deeply hurt under the beneficent guise of constructive criticism. Being on the receiving end of any criticism hurts. That's why it's best to replace criticism with kindness.

| EXUDE ENERGY |

Iron rusts from disuse; even so does inaction sap the vigor of the mind.
—Leonardo da Vinci

Have you ever watched little kids bounce out of bed and race to the tree on Christmas morning, usually at an hour most adults would consider obscene? Contrast that with the moans, groans, and assorted contortions some older adults exhibit just getting out of a chair.

Now I'm not suggesting that arthritic joints aren't uncomfortable, but moaning and groaning does not facilitate the process. If anything it intensifies the perception of pain. Take a moment and think about your reaction to people who are bright and energetic. Unless you're in an unusually morose mood, you probably find energetic people appealing. High-energy people feel good about themselves and in turn, most people feel good about them. But what if you—or your patients—don't feel energetic? What do you do when you feel tired and worn out?

> HIGH-ENERGY PEOPLE FEEL GOOD ABOUT THEMSELVES AND IN TURN, MOST PEOPLE FEEL GOOD ABOUT THEM.

The first step is to get a thorough medical evaluation to rule out some underlying illness. Anemia, thyroid disorders, diabetes, heart disease and long list of other conditions can drain energy from the most upbeat individual.

QUICK TIP FROM DR. O

AFTER ELIMINATING CONCERNS ABOUT A SERIOUS ILLNESS, THERE ARE SEVERAL WAYS TO BEEF UP ENERGY:

* GET ENOUGH REST. NO ONE CAN BE ENERGETIC WHEN THEY'RE CHRONICALLY SLEEP DEPRIVED.

* LEARN TO LIKE ACTIVITY. THE BEST WAY TO BANISH THE BLAHS IS TO GET UP AND GET GOING.

* BY EATING RIGHT AND LIGHT, YOU'LL SHED THE EXTRA POUNDS THAT MAKE YOU FEEL SLUGGISH.

* RELEASE STRESS. PENT UP STRESS AND TENSION CAN LEAD TO CHRONIC EXHAUSTION. DEVELOP A RELIABLE RELEASE VALVE AND USE IT REGULARLY.

* HAVE SOME FUN. WE ALL FIND OURSELVES IN A RUT FROM TIME TO TIME, AND RUTS ARE TIRING. HAVING FUN IS ENERGIZING.

There is one last step you and your patients can take to act energetic. That's right, acting like you feel great makes it come true. Walk faster, talk faster and smile. You'll confuse your brain long enough to start feeling genuinely energetic!

| CELEBRATE YOUR SOCIAL LIFE |

| OPEN YOURSELF TO OPTIMISM |

Twixt the optimist and the pessimist
The difference is droll:
The optimist sees the doughnut
But the pessimist sees the hole.
—McLandburgh Wilson

Successful agers consistently focus on the doughnut, not the hole. They don't waste time worrying about the love, money, time or opportunities they've lost. They look forward to the possibilities inherent in each new day. Youthful people fully expect life to get better at every turn.

A 2002 study published in the Mayo Clinic Proceedings backs up the power of optimism. According to the study, people who scored high on optimism had a 50% lower risk of early death than those who were more pessimistic.

Does that mean that youthful people are addicted to the silly sort of positive thinking promoted by some pop-psychologists? The answer is a resounding "no!" Healthy optimism doesn't deny that problems and frustrations exist. Healthy optimism acknowledges the problem but concentrates on possible solutions. Optimism is a much healthier, happier approach to life because we often get what we expect.

| DO UNTO OTHERS |

Do unto others what you would have them do unto you.
–Jesus, Luke 6:31

If there were ever a single secret to successful living surely it's contained in that quote. The vast majority of our personal, national, and global problems could be solved if we practiced that time-honored advice. Well, none of us can control behavior on a national or global scale, but we can control our own. How could we change our lives if we consistently treated other people well?

I'm awestruck to think how my own life would be transformed if I were always loving, patient, kind, tolerant, generous, and non-judgmental. When I'm happy, healthy, rested, and relaxed, those virtues come fairly easily. But I'm not always happy, healthy, rested, and relaxed. Perhaps you

> HOW COULD WE CHANGE OUR LIVES IF WE CONSISTENTLY TREATED OTHER PEOPLE WELL?

| CELEBRATE YOUR SOCIAL LIFE |

can relate. Somehow the practice of those noble virtues is considerably more challenging when depression, illness, fatigue, or stress intervenes.

None of us get through life without our share of difficulties and disappointments. And during the difficult times we tend to focus on our own pain with remarkable acuity. I can remember making nursing home rounds one day when I was tense and feeling perfectly miserable. The thought of listening to one more patient recite their litany of complaints was almost more than I could bear. But the next patient I saw didn't offer a single complaint. She was a lovely 92-year-old lady with a saintly disposition. To this day I'm convinced she read my mind. "Sit down, dear," she said as I walked in the room. "You look like it's been a long day." I was disappointed that my appearance was so transparent. "It must be exhausting taking care of old people all day long. I bet you get tired of hearing their complaints."

> NONE OF US GET THROUGH LIFE WITHOUT OUR SHARE OF DIFFICULTIES AND DISAPPOINTMENTS.

I must have looked positively dumbfounded as she continued. "I get tired of hearing the other residents here complain but I know they're just lonely and looking for a little sympathy." By this time I thought I saw a halo forming over her head. "Don't you let them drain you though, dear. You get some rest and have a life of your own while you're still young. You deserve to be happy."

I'm sure that wonderful woman had no idea how much her selfless words touched me. She could have recited a long list of complaints but she didn't. She was more concerned about my fatigue. She taught me a vital lesson about living by the Golden Rule. And I'll never forget it.

| INTERACT WITH ALL AGES |

Variety's the very spice of life.
–William Cowper

Millions of retirees congregate in communities where the uniformity of age is downright stifling. And, more often than not, such communities often reflect an oppressive uniformity of culture, religion, education and background. Boring... there's nothing conducive to personal growth and development in an environment that segregates people according to age.

The superstars of successful aging interact with people of all ages. They can color with a little kid or commiserate with a centenarian. They appreciate the best each generation has to offer. It has been noticed over the centuries that we tend to become like the people with whom we associate. So with whom are you associating? Bright, youthful, dynamic people, the movers and shakers, geniuses and poets? Or the sour old poops of your corner of the world? Enjoy reminiscing with colleagues and cronies, but interact with all ages. You'll find more people will want to interact with you.

| COMPLAIN NO MORE |

When a member of my family complains to me of having bitten his tongue, pinched a finger, or the like, he does not get the sympathy he hopes for but instead the question: "Why did you do that?"
—Sigmund Freud

Have you ever gone to a dinner party or reception of sorts and regretted asking someone "How are you?" All you wanted to hear was, "Fine, thanks. And how are you?" But instead you endured an avalanche of awful agonies and miserable misfortunes. You hoped in vain that some kind stranger would interrupt and bring a merciful end to a one-way conversation. But alas, the soliloquy of complaints continued. Finally, in desperation you offer a silent prayer of petition, "Please, God, make this person go away!"

I can't help but notice that complaining is a way of life for many folks as they age. Not that youth provides immunity from whining.

> A HAPPY LIFE FILLED WITH LOVING FRIENDS AND FAMILY OFTEN RESULTS WHEN YOU QUIT COMPLAINING.

Some teenagers have elevated complaining to an art form. But 50, 60, or 70 years of living can convince some people they've "earned the right" to complain. The problem is, no one likes listening to someone else's complaints. Complainers end up very lonely.

The truth is that a happy life filled with loving friends and family often results when you quit complaining. And that's a sensational secret of successful aging!

CHAPTER 7

FIRM UP YOUR FINANCES

Happiness seems to require a modicum of external prosperity.
—*Aristotle*

Whenever I speak on successful aging I address the issue of financial security. It invariably elicits raised eyebrows and puzzled expressions. Why is a doctor talking about finances instead of physiology? It's simple. There's a colossal difference between growing old and rich versus growing old and poor. Rich old people are, for the most part, happier and healthier than poor old people. You won't hear this broadcast on the evening news because it's not considered politically correct to be that blunt. But the premise remains true. Money can't guarantee great health or perfect bliss but it can certainly solve a lot of life's problems. Regardless of your present age, pay careful attention to the "secrets" in this chapter. Firming up your finances is a crucial step in successful living!

| ADJUST YOUR ATTITUDE |

Every man takes the limits of his own field of vision for the limits of the world.
—Schopenhauer

Analyzing your attitude toward money is crucial because it has a tremendous impact on the quality of life. And yet, many

QUICK TIP FROM DR. O

FOR EXAMPLE, HOW OFTEN HAVE YOU HEARD AND ACCEPTED STATEMENTS LIKE THESE:

* MONEY IS THE ROOT OF ALL EVIL

* A PENNY SAVED IS A PENNY EARNED

* RICH PEOPLE TAKE ADVANTAGE OF POOR PEOPLE

* TAKE CARE OF THE PENNIES AND THE DOLLARS WILL TAKE CARE OF THEMSELVES

* IF YOU MAKE MONEY YOU'LL JUST HAVE TO PAY MORE TAXES

* RICH PEOPLE HAVE MORE TO WORRY ABOUT

of us plod through the years with some rather dubious ideas about money ruminating through our minds.

You can probably add many others to the list. The point is acceptance of and belief in any of these statements is a great way to stay broke! St. Paul didn't call money the root of all evil. He said, "The love of money is the root of all evil." Big difference. When I didn't have any money, I worked 100 hours a week chasing it and nearly ruined my health for good. Most people demonstrate a love of money when they don't have enough of it. Where does crime and violence run rampant, in beautiful, affluent neighborhoods or in the slums and ghettos? Money is not the problem. The lack of money breeds a lust for it that leads to the worst kinds of evil.

A penny saved is a penny earned. Now there's an expansive concept. Are there any folks who make a production out of saving pennies? Do they have immense visionary insight? Highly unlikely. The penny pinchers of the world are usually pitiful pea brained people who contribute precious little to others.

And what about rich people taking advantage of the poor? No doubt that's happened throughout history. But the vast majority of hospitals, churches, libraries, museums, and charities exist because people shared their abundance. Money is neither good nor bad. It merely reflects the character of the person who has it.

When you earn more, you will be in a higher tax bracket, but is investing all that money really a headache? It's amazing that people worry about these things when they're broke and actually use them as an excuse not to earn more. A positive, creative, and constructive attitude toward money is worth its weight in gold.

| MAXIMIZE YOUR SKILLS |

Skills and confidence are an unconquered army.
—George Herbert

Many people let their education come to a grinding halt at some graduation ceremony. Then they wonder why their paycheck never seems to keep up with their needs.

Our world is changing at a dizzying rate. And anyone who wants to enjoy financial security will need to keep up. It's been said that knowledge is power, but that's not entirely true. Applied knowledge is power because people will always pay for results. Skills learned in 1967 may not be useful in 2007. But don't fall into the trap of thinking some business course or another degree will be a ticket to financial freedom. That approach may earn an extra $100.00 month, a rather feeble return on the investment. A far better approach is to find someone who's already living your dream and model his or her behavior. It's important to find a mentor, read like crazy, and develop good people skills.

Don't think this advice is just for 20-year-olds! No one ever has so many birthdays they can't learn something new.

QUICK TIP FROM DR. O

IT'S NEVER TOO LATE TO TACKLE A NEW SET OF SKILLS. CONSIDER THIS:

* THOMAS EDISON LAUNCHED THE CAMPAIGN TO CREATE THE NAVAL RESEARCH LABORATORY AT AGE 73.

* BENJAMIN FRANKLIN EFFECTED THE COMPROMISE THAT LED TO THE DEVELOPMENT AND ACCEPTANCE OF THE CONSTITUTION AT AGE 81.

* CLAUDE MONET BEGAN HIS FAMOUS WATER LILY PAINTINGS WHEN HE WAS 73.

| Minimize Your Bills |

Debt is the worst poverty
−Thomas Fuller

Imagine you're 90 years old. Imagine further that your savings are meager, you don't own your home, and you can't pay your medical bills. It's not a comforting scenario. How different life is at 90 or any other age, if you are completely debt free.

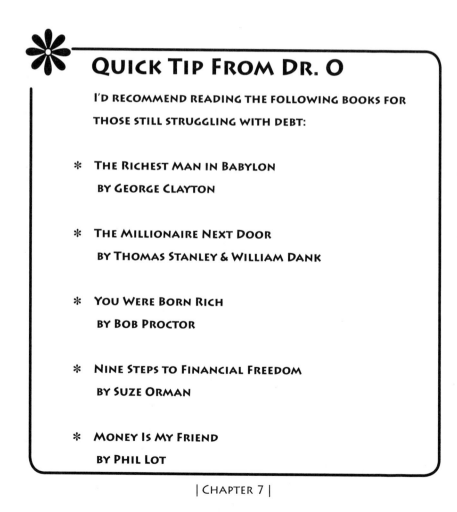

Quick Tip From Dr. O

I'd recommend reading the following books for those still struggling with debt:

* **The Richest Man in Babylon**
  by George Clayton

* **The Millionaire Next Door**
  by Thomas Stanley & William Dank

* **You Were Born Rich**
  by Bob Proctor

* **Nine Steps to Financial Freedom**
  by Suze Orman

* **Money Is My Friend**
  by Phil Lot

✱ Quick Tip From Dr. O

There are several highly effective strategies for reducing and eventually eliminating debt. Practice them faithfully:

✱ Do not spend more than you earn. Period.

✱ If you can't payoff your credit card balance each month, you're spending beyond your means. Cut up the credit cards until you learn how to handle them properly.

✱ Keep your present car as long as possible. Never take out a new car loan for more than 3 years. Ideally, you should pay cash-and you can if you follow these principles.

✱ Get the shortest home mortgage possible. A 15-year mortgage does not require twice the monthly payment of a 30-year mortgage. The increase in monthly payment is modest but you'll save $60,000 to well over $100,000 over the life of the loan.

✱ Apply 10% of your monthly net income toward debt reduction.

✱ Stop wasting money on cigarettes, alcohol, junk food, and unnecessary incidentals.

✱ Pay your bills promptly. Avoid late fees.

✱ Save 10% of your monthly income and pay yourself first.

No one can age successfully crushed by the weight of endless unpaid bills and debt.

> ...THE GREATEST REWARDS HAVE ALWAYS GONE TO THOSE WILLING TO BE BOLD AND TAKE RISKS.

| LEARN HOW TO EARN |

So much is man worth as he esteems himself.
—Rabelais

From the dawn of civilization the greatest rewards have always gone to those willing to be bold and take risks.

If you're really serious about successful aging here's a tip: ignore the negative people out there, the sour old poops that know what won't work. Develop a dream and pursue it. Most people have more talents than they realize and tremendous potential that's yet to be tapped. Older people have skills and wisdom and experience someone somewhere would be willing to pay for. Don't sell yourself short.

| INVEST WITH ZEST |

If a little does not go, much cash will not come.
—Chinese proverb

Here are some crucial questions for retaining and growing your nest egg. Are your assets properly protected with appropriate insurance? Are your investments well positioned for security and growth? The answers will determine, to a very great extent, just how golden those golden years will be.

Regardless of age, it's good to save at least 10% of monthly income. Don't worry about stocks and bonds until you've set aside 6–12 months of living expenses in a savings account or preferably a money market fund. Do not, repeat, and do not wait to save money until the bills are paid. That approach will keep anyone living paycheck to paycheck. Remember that the goal is financial independence.

Once you've saved 12 months of living expenses, begin investing for growth. People's needs will vary as they age, but some money should be invested in reasonably stable stocks and mutual funds. Read about the financial markets, learn how to invest wisely. Don't leave these decisions in the hands of strangers and "experts." It's wise to become an expert on your own money, because you'll wind up with more of it in the end.

| ENJOY BEING GENEROUS |

Give and it shall be given unto you. Good measure, pressed down, shaken together, running over shall men pour into your bosom.
—*Jesus, Luke 7:38*

No doubt you've heard it said, "God loves a cheerful giver." Well, so does everyone else. The tightwads of the world are neither personally fulfilled nor much fun to be with. But how, you may ask, can generosity improve financial status? The truth is generosity has an uncanny way of catching up with you. Many folks from a Judeo-Christian background are at least aware of the concept of tithing. It was described in the Old Testament as the key to opening the windows of heaven. But every major religion of the world extols the virtue and benefits of being generous. Muslims are to provide gracious hospitality to travelers, even if they are total strangers. It's considered a sacred duty. Similar concepts are promoted in Hindu and Buddhist cultures.

> NO ONE CAN OUTGIVE GOD.

Emerson described the benefits of being generous in his classic essay, "The Law of Compensation." Simply put, the universe recognizes, records and rewards generosity. Whatever you give, whether it's time, money, work, or material, will eventually come back to you. The rewards of being generous spill over into every facet of life. Wealth can be accumulated by penny pinching, scrimping and hoarding a la Scrooge. But that approach to money eventually impoverishes the heart and soul. Misers have precious few friends and even less fun as they go through life. It's tough to love a tightwad. They don't even like themselves!

If the mere thought of being more generous fills you with fear, just relax. Try it for a month or two. Emerson was right. So was Jesus. No one can outgive God.

| ATTRACT ABUNDANCE |

As a man thinketh in his heart, so is he.
—Proverbs 23:7

All this talk about money makes some people terribly nervous. And yet, the lack of money is probably responsible for more marital spats, family arguments, sleepless nights and despair than any other issue. I've never heard a couple fight like this: "Frank, I just can't stand this house another minute! I'm sick and tired of all these hundred dollar bills stacked up everywhere. For crying out loud! Can't you do something about it?"

As a friend of mine says, "Money can't buy you happiness but it will bring you the kind of misery you can thoroughly enjoy!" There is a fundamental principle of the universe that very few people are taught. Most people scoff at it when they do stumble upon it. But the most brilliant sages throughout human history have recognized its truth. You become what you think about.

Don't dwell on poverty, lack, scarcity, and insufficiency. Instead, cultivate thoughts of prosperity, abundance, and wealth. It's really a matter of disciplining your thought process. There's nothing natural or spontaneous about this. The idea is to consciously cultivate a mindset of abundance. The world, the media, and most of your broke relatives will do their darndest to convince you otherwise. They'll extol the virtues of being "realistic." Focus like a laser on all the good things you desire: health, wealth, happiness, love. An abundant mindset will eventually bring far more of your dreams into being than "realism" ever will. As an old Jewish friend of mine used to say, "At least it couldn't hurt!"

> "MONEY CAN'T BUY YOU HAPPINESS BUT IT WILL BRING YOU THE KIND OF MISERY YOU CAN THOROUGHLY ENJOY!"

CHAPTER 8 SEARCHING FOR YOUR SPIRIT

The tragedy of man is what dies inside himself while he still lives.

—Albert Schweitzer

There are people who simply age prematurely, and become mere shells of their former selves. The twinkle in their eyes is long gone and the emptiness of their existence borders on painful. They may profess to be profoundly religious but as Luke Skywalker might say, "The Force is not with them." Millions of people fall into the abyss of apathy in their teens and twenties and never discover a way out. Their spirit withers and dies and waits years for their body to catch up. It is, as Albert Schweitzer declared, the tragedy of man.

The opposite image is inspiring, indeed. Can any lover of classical music erase the image of Vladimir Horowitz, frail and feeble in his late 80's, transforming himself on a Moscow stage in a passionate display of pianistic virtuosity? Spellbound concertgoers sat breathlessly anticipating each note, and wishing it could go on forever. The miraculous spark of the human spirit can transform even the most beleaguered body into a joyful wonder.

But there is a catch. The human spirit requires cultivation. It must be protected and nurtured, which is no small feat in an age of fax machines and cellular phones. The "secrets" that follow will help you search for that sacred part within, your spirit.

| SEEK SERENITY |

Of one thing I am certain, the body is not the measure of healing - peace is the measure.
—George Melton

Peace. Tranquility. Serenity. These are qualities essential for health and happiness. Have you ever noticed how dreadful you feel (and look) when conflict, stress, and strife dominate your life? This can present a challenge, since conflict, stress, and strife appear to be part of the human condition.

How any busy, responsible person can seek serenity in the midst of modern day mayhem may seem a mystery. If peace and serenity are going to grace our lives we need to find them within.

Of course, there are a few people and places you may want to avoid like bars, casinos, shopping malls on weekends,

❋ QUICK TIP FROM DR. O

AS FAR AS I CAN TELL THERE ARE SEVERAL SERENITY SEEKING STRATEGIES THAT HAVE BEEN SUCCESSFULLY EMPLOYED BY A WIDE VARIETY OF SAGES OVER THE CENTURIES. HERE ARE A FEW OF MY FAVORITES:

* TURN OFF THE TV.

* KEEP IT OFF; THIS IS THE 21ST CENTURY VERSION OF OBSERVING THE MONASTIC TRADITION OF THE GRAND SILENCE.

* VISIT A CHURCH OR TEMPLE WHEN NO ONE ELSE IS AROUND.

* WATCH A SUNSET.

* TAKE A FEW DEEP BREATHS.

* SIT NEAR A FOUNTAIN.

* SPEND TIME IN A GARDEN.

* TAKE A WALK IN THE WOODS.

* DIM THE LIGHTS.

* LISTEN TO WIND CHIMES.

* STARE AT THE STARS.

* WATCH THE SUN COME UP.

negative neighbors, gossips, and contentious relatives. When you external world calms down, you'll have a much better chance of finding the calm within. Trust me. It's better than anything on TV.

| PRAY PEACEFULLY |

I have found power in the mysteries of thought.
—Euripides

The best prayer comes from the heart. It is natural. It is spontaneous. And it is blissfully nondenominational. The New American Dictionary defines prayer as "a reverent petition made to a deity" or "any act of communion with God." Now there's a powerful concept—an act of communion with God. That seems infinitely more inspiring than the sort of puny pleading and spiritual plea-bargaining that often passes for prayer.

In Galatians 5:22–23, St. Paul states, "The fruit of the spirit is love, joy, peace, patience, kindness, goodness,

THE BEST PRAYER COMES FROM
THE HEART. IT IS NATURAL.

| CHAPTER 8 |

faithfulness, gentleness, and self control." Personal experience over the years has convinced me that's true. But, in fact, medical research has validated Paul's observation. Of course, modern science doesn't usually deal with concepts like love, joy, peace, and patience, but depression (which can be thought of as the lack of love, joy, and peace) has been studied extensively. Leave it to modern medicine to focus on the negative.

In any event, a large study conducted at the Durham Veterans Administration Hospital in North Carolina in 1988 found that men who used religious behaviors to cope were less likely to be depressed during their initial hospital stay and less likely to become depressed if hospitalized in the future. This is significant indeed! Depression has a devastating effect on older people. Not only does it rob them of happiness, joy, and meaning in life, but it interferes with good medical care, frequently shortens life expectancy, and costs huge sums of money to treat.

Studies also show that spirituality can benefit people with heart disease and those trying to lose weight. In a 2001 study, participants in Dr. Dean Ornish's Lifestyle Heart Trial were given the "Spiritual Orientation Inventory." The lowest spirituality scores predicted progression of heart disease and greater coronary artery obstruction over a four-year-period. "This study suggests that the degree of spiritual well-being may be an important factor in the development of coronary artery disease," the researchers wrote in their abstract.

Perhaps the most dramatic study on the medical effects of prayer was conducted in the coronary care unit at San Francisco General Hospital and reported in the Southern Medical Journal in July 1988. A computer assigned 393 patients into two groups. People in home prayer groups prayed for one group of patients. The other group of patients received no special prayer. The study was a randomized, double blind project, which meant that neither the patients nor nurses nor the doctors knew who was in which group. The patients who were prayed for experienced results that were interesting to say the least: they were five times less likely than the control group to require antibiotics; and three times less likely to develop pulmonary edema. None of the prayed-for patients required mechanical ventilation while 12 patients in the control group did. Finally, fewer of the prayed-for patients died although the difference was not statistically significant. As you might imagine, such a study drew more than its share of criticism.

Another recent study published in the Annals of Internal Medicine added more research evidence supporting the impact of prayer. In the study, volunteers prayed for 484 cardiac patients. In the end, the "prayed for" group had fewer complications, used fewer drugs, and fared better than the control group.

The power of prayer remains a fascinating mystery. Even the renowned physician Sir William Osler felt compelled to admit, "Nothing in life is more wonderful than faith—the one great moving force that we can neither weigh in the balance nor test in the crucible." If folks as diverse as Euripides and Sir William Osler thought prayer were a good idea, it just might be worth considering today.

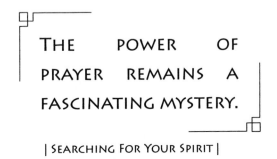

THE POWER OF PRAYER REMAINS A FASCINATING MYSTERY.

| SEARCHING FOR YOUR SPIRIT |

| REFLECT REGULARLY |

The unexamined life is not worth living.
—Socrates

There's no way to get around it. Reflection is crucial for spiritual development. But reflection requires periodic intervals of calmness and quiet. That's a challenge for most folks in our culture. It's tough to reflect or meditate on the mysteries of life when two TV's, two radios and video games are blaring. And yet as the saying goes, those who fail to learn from the past are doomed to repeat it. I suspect that's exactly what happens to people with endless tales of woe. They simply don't take time to reflect on the choices they've made and take corrective action.

The truth is, most ships and jets are frequently off course by tiny increments. They receive data constantly, however, that allows them to adjust course minute to minute. If they didn't, a lot of tourists headed for Hawaii would end up in the Bering Straits.

REFLECTION REQUIRES PERIODIC INTERVALS OF CALMNESS AND QUIET.

One of the most vital secrets of successful aging I've ever learned is contained in this simple concept of navigational correction. Ships and jets need some version of a high-tech computer assisted compass. People need quiet time and reflection. By reflecting on our successes and failures, we can figure out what worked and what didn't.

Of course, applying that insight then becomes critical. But the insight comes first. Take time to reflect regularly on your life. Review the failures and successes. Think about things you might have done differently. Then do them differently. That's what progress is all about, professionally, physically, emotionally, or spiritually. Each year can be better than the last, but only when we take time to examine the past.

| SAVOR SOLITUDE |

In Genesis it says that it is not good for a man
to be alone, but sometimes it's a great relief.
–John Barrymore

Have you ever met anyone who's terrified of being alone? They'd do almost anything to avoid hearing the sound of silence.

Desperate for distraction they race around in a constant frenzy, hoping other people will entertain them. People like that are rarely content. They seldom accomplish anything significant because they don't make time to hear themselves think. As Thomas Edison said, "The best thinking has been done in solitude. The worst has been done in turmoil." No argument there. Creative genius thrives on solitude. So do wisdom, common sense, good judgement and decision-making.

Many folks find old age a time of terrifying loneliness. The progressive loss of friends and family is a sad but inevitable fact of life. Unfortunately, the individual who has never taken time to befriend himself in solitude will almost certainly feel abandoned as the years progress. It's so much easier and infinitely more productive to cultivate contented solitude an hour or two at a time, starting right now. As Arthur Brisbane recommended, "Get away from the crowd when you can. Keep yourself to yourself, if only for a few hours daily." You'll see an increase in contentment and creativity, and it won't cost a dime. Now that's a bargain!

| FORGIVE FREELY |

*Without forgiveness life is governed by an
endless cycle of resentment and retaliation.*
—Roberto Assagioli

What could be worse than a bitter old age filled with resentment? Not much. And yet millions of people cling

> "TO BE WRONGED IS NOTHING UNLESS YOU CONTINUE TO REMEMBER IT."

tenaciously to their pet peeves and grudges till they go to their graves, no doubt griping all the way. They'll fuss and fume for a lifetime over some perceived outrage they suffered at the hands of a relative or acquaintance turned villain. The ironic thing is, the "villain" in question quite often has no inkling of their outrageous offense and may even have died years ago. Invariably some sanctimonious so-and-so will deign to announce, "I can forgive, but I'll never forget!" Odd that none of the great spiritual masters over the centuries shared that sentiment. As Confucius said, "To be wronged is nothing unless you continue to remember it."

Regardless of your religious convictions or lack thereof, it's tough to think of any person more grievously wronged than Jesus. Tortured and crucified despite being found innocent, He forgave his tormentors at the peak of his agony.

No, there's a reason every major religion in the world extols the need for forgiveness. Apart

...IT'S TOUGH TO THINK OF ANY PERSON MORE GRIEVOUSLY WRONGED THAN JESUS.

from whatever forgiveness may do for a person's spiritual well being, it does extraordinary things for one's psychological well being. There is something wonderfully and mysteriously liberating about true forgiveness. It releases us from the psychological quicksand of anger and resentment. And I can't think of any disease that ages a person faster than chronic anger and resentment.

In fact, scientific studies have shown the beneficial effects of forgiveness on health. In a study published in the Journal of Behavioral Medicine in 2003, 108 college students participated in two interviews about personal betrayals they had experienced. Measures of forgiving personality were taken as well as symptoms of stress, hostility, empathy and illness. Blood pressure, EMG and skin conductance were monitored. As it turned out, those who showed the most forgiveness had lower blood pressure levels, lower heart rate, and less reactivity to stress.

Instead of stewing about some injury or offense you've endured, let go of it. Forgive and forget. It's not as hard as we make it seem. The rewards of forgiveness are much richer than those of resentment.

| LOVE LAVISHLY |

People who are sensible about love are incapable of it.
—Douglas Yates

Picture yourself at age 80. Are you surrounded by loyal friends and loving family members? Do you have a twinkle in your eyes and a smile on your face? Or are you isolated, alone and depressed? The choice is, to a large extent, up to each of us. The more love and affection we shower on others, the more our own lives are enriched.

Every day I deal with folks who have spent a lifetime waiting for other people to declare their undying love and affection. They are invariably depressed, disillusioned, and disappointed. But they lack insight into their loneliness. Perhaps they never took the time to learn the Law of Compensation. Simply put, whatever we put out into the universe eventually comes back to us. Give love, encouragement, praise, and gratitude to others and eventually you'll be the happy recipient of the same.

Sound too simple? It's easy to resort to cynicism in our culture. For decades we've been told to look out for number one, do unto others before they do unto you, get it while the getting's good, and follow the precepts of the "me generation." There's only one problem with that approach to life. It doesn't bring happiness. It may, in the short run, make you richer, stronger, and more powerful. But it will not make you loved, respected, and admired. And, so far, I haven't met anyone who could be truly happy without love, respect, and at least a little admiration.

So how loving should one be? Isn't it wise to exercise a little prudence where love is concerned? After all, talk shows abound with the woes of women who "love too much." I suppose there is such a thing as misguided love, but true, genuine, sincere love is capable of great sacrifice and extravagance. Prudence is not a characteristic of great love. As Samuel Johnson said, "Prudence keeps life safe, but does not often make it happy." An even wiser man once said, "No one has greater love than this – that he lay down his life for his friends." Nothing prudent about that. But there must be something to it because it's withstood the test of time. So think about the special people you love. Do you take them for granted or shower them with affection, encouragement, and praise? Indulge them. Pamper them. Be extravagant now and then. You'll increase the flow of love and happiness in the world and eventually it will come back to you.

I HAVEN'T MET ANYONE WHO COULD BE TRULY HAPPY WITHOUT LOVE, RESPECT, AND AT LEAST A LITTLE ADMIRATION.

| PURSUE YOUR PURPOSE |

*This is the true joy in life, the being used for a purpose recognized by
yourself as a mighty one; the being thoroughly worn out before you
are thrown on the scrap heap; the being a force of nature instead of
a feverish little clod of ailments and grievances complaining that
the world will not devote itself to making you happy.*
—George Bernard Shaw

I love that quote. If everyone acted on that principle the entire
human race would take a quantum leap forward. The question
is, have you thought about your purpose in life? Not your
profession or career or job title. Being Senior Vice President
of Such and Such is not a suitable life purpose for anyone.
The reason is simple if unsettling. Two days after you're dead
someone else will be appointed Acting Senior Vice President
of Such and Such. And if you have failed to devote yourself to
a mighty and meaningful purpose apart from a job title, your
life will have made frighteningly little difference in the world.

It's tragic to realize the vast majority of people go to
their graves having never discovered their true purpose in life.
So why are you here? Perhaps your purpose is to teach, uplift,
or encourage other people. Maybe your role is to bring love,

laughter, or kindness to your fellow man. If you're a nurse or a doctor, do you really devote yourself to restoring health and relieving suffering? If you're a teacher, do you really strive to bring out the best in others? If you function in the business world, are you really dedicated to making life better for your customers and clients?

When we become crystal clear on our true purpose in life, everything changes. Our perspective deepens and expands. Our level of energy and enthusiasm increases. Our efficiency and effectiveness reach new heights. We're no longer defined by redundant job descriptions and arbitrary titles. The really wonderful thing is, when you know your true life's purpose, you never really retire.

When your life has true purpose, it will be abundantly clear on that last day that you were infinitely more than a "feverish little clod of ailments and grievances." You will have been a force of nature devoted to a mighty purpose. And the love and joy you will have created in the process will endure forever in the hearts of those your life has touched.

CHAPTER 9 ENJOYING YOUR LIFE

There is more to life than increasing its speed.

–Gandhi

Could there be a more crucial concept than that as we explore the 21st century? In recent years, a fast, furious and frenetic lifestyle has left everyone from toddlers to 92-year-olds exhausted. Three year olds can no longer sit quietly doing shoe box art with Captain Kangaroo. No, in order to keep up and compete with all the other three-year-olds, they're carted off to gymnastics, tumbling, swimming classes and pre-pre-school all before noon. No wonder they're cranky and hyperactive the rest of the day. The same preposterous pace is sustained through grade school, high school, college, and beyond. Working mothers juggle more activities than six performers in a circus act. And increasing numbers of retired folks feel compelled to re-enter the rat race. The sad part is, very few of them are really having fun.

Is fun such a big deal in the aging process? I think so. In fact, experience has convinced me that having fun is right up there with good nutrition and exercise. I wouldn't be surprised, if, in 50 years, science showed us that enjoying life is every bit as important as genetics. Folks could visit their doctor, have their blood pressure and cholesterol levels checked and then have their enjoyment quotient analyzed. People all over the planet would then have a new entity to describe themselves-the E.Q. I can see it now. The E.Q. could give rise to a whole new cadre of service organizations, clubs, and classes. It's even conceivable that one day people might go to a party and discuss their Enjoyment Quotient instead of all their woes and miseries. Okay, I confess that's overly optimistic. But wouldn't it be wonderful if we could all slow down enough to appreciate being alive?

It frightens me to realize how many people I've encountered or heard about who are literally tired of being alive. How sad to think so many of us are too busy living to enjoy life. Maybe it's time for the whole human race to ease up on the accelerator and enjoy the blessings we do have. Gandhi was right. There's a lot more to life than increasing its speed. We could slow down and increase our enjoyment.

> HOW SAD TO THINK SO MANY OF US ARE TOO BUSY LIVING TO ENJOY LIFE.

| MAKE MEALS AN EVENT |

The discovery of a new dish does more for human happiness than the discovery of a new star.
—Jean-Anthelme Brillat-Savarin

No doubt that sentiment would garner an argument from the astronomers out there. But you get the point. Human beings crave variety and newness in taste sensations, and yet most of us look forward to that traditional Thanksgiving feast. I want mashed potatoes and gravy with my turkey and stuffing. Potatoes nouveau simply won't do the trick. Is there more behind this preference than being finicky? Yes there is. In an age when tradition and ritual have all but disappeared, familiar foods can be uniquely comforting.

The number of families who sit down together for dinner each night is distressingly small. Dinner for individual family members is often as varied as a Big Mac eaten on the run, a piece of re-warmed pizza consumed while standing in front of the kitchen sink, and a TV dinner inhaled while watching reruns of "Friends."

> THE NUMBER OF FAMILIES WHO SIT DOWN TOGETHER FOR DINNER EACH NIGHT IS DISTRESSINGLY SMALL.

This sort of on-the-go grazing is uniquely and pathetically American. Folks in European and Asian cultures make virtually every meal an event. Italians spend two hours lingering over lunch after which the entire country takes a nap. They even serve beer and wine in their hospital cafeterias since no one in their right mind would make life and death decisions on an empty stomach. Apparently their patients and families don't mind much since they have a little vino with lunch, too. Standard operating procedure in many Asian businesses is a well-prepared leisurely lunch followed by a meditation period or corporate naptime. Compare that with the neurotic American lunch practice of wolfing down a sandwich while seated in a conference room as someone drones on about P & L statements, potential downsizing, or (as is often the case in medical circles) seasonal varieties of infectious diarrhea.

Yes, Americans have a real knack for massacring an otherwise enjoyable meal. You'd think we'd be bright enough to realize that the way we eat is doing us in as much as what we eat. There's no shortage of fat in diets of the French, Italians, and Greeks. It's just that they slow down and relax long enough to enjoy it. Make at least one meal a day an event. I'll lay odds you'll live longer. And even if you don't, at least you'll live happy.

| THE SCIENCE BEHIND BUBBLE BATHS |

Calgon, take me away.
—Stressed out woman in a commercial

We're getting a bit personal here, but are your hygiene habits strictly utilitarian? They are for the most frazzled folks in our culture. Get up, get clean, and get out the door is typical of the daily drudgery many of us endure. I'd be hard pressed to think of one working mother I know who has the time or freedom to luxuriate in a bubble bath more than once every decade or so. That's unfortunate since the mere act of relaxing in a bubble bath combines three of nature's most rejuvenating elements: water, heat, and soothing aromas. For thousands of years the therapeutic effects of these elements were extolled in the cultures of Japan, China, Greece, Egypt, India and Rome. In fact, for centuries perfumes and medicines were considered practically interchangeable.

American medical culture often scoffs at the very notion of aromatherapy, but perhaps we should reconsider. In Germany, patients have access to "forest therapy" during which a variety of floral and herbal vapors are inhaled. The high-powered Japanese corporate structure has designed office buildings with ventilation systems that pipe in scents like citrus, mint, and evergreen. The choice of aroma is strategically chosen to perk people up in the morning and calm them down at the end of the day. We may chuckle, but at least aromatherapy is cheaper and less addicting than Xanax.

But let's not over look the extraordinary effect of heat on the human body. There's a reason so many people

> A LONG LEISURELY BUBBLE BATH DOES WONDERS FOR THE SOUL AND PSYCHE.

enjoy sitting in saunas, hot tubs, and steam baths. A European study showed that sitting in a sauna for 30 minutes doubled the production of endorphins, those wonderful natural chemicals that make us feel good. A German study of children in kindergarten demonstrated a dramatic reduction in colds and ear infections when children took a weekly sauna.

Science notwithstanding, a long leisurely bubble bath does wonders for the soul and psyche. It simply makes you feel better. Given the relentless stress of modern life, it makes sense to slow down long enough for a nice hot bath. As the lady in the Calgon commercial proclaimed, "Take me away from all this!" A little escapism is good for the soul. Isn't it amazing what you can learn from a commercial?

| WALK NEAR WATER |

Water, thou hast no taste, no color, no odor; canst not be defined, art relished while ever mysterious. Not necessary to life, but rather life itself, thou fillest us with a gratification that exceeds the delights of the senses.
—Saint Exupery

That's an elegant way of saying, "Isn't water wonderful!" And indeed, it is. Anyone who has stood in awe watching the

> ...A MAJORITY OF "SUCCESSFUL AGERS" SPENT SIGNIFICANT PERIODS OF TIME NEAR WATER.

power of Niagara Falls, the vastness of the Pacific Ocean, or the tranquility of the Caribbean, has experienced the nearly hypnotic effect of water on the human heart. We just can't seem to get enough of it. But does it really have an impact on the aging process? Many people believe it does. Research done by Dr. Kenneth Pelletier showed that a majority of "successful agers" spent significant periods of time near water. Not that living on the beach is a prerequisite for hitting age 100 in good health. But it certainly seems to help. Being near water simply allows us to slow down, calm down, and enjoy being alive.

As we've increased the pace of life in the twentieth century, we've suppressed our instincts for spontaneous enjoyment. Why else would so many folks today admit or boast about the fact that the first four or five days of a vacation are spent trying to unwind enough to have fun? We're so run down, uptight, and stressed out we have to "practice" relaxation.

Fortunately, the mere presence of water seems to facilitate the entire process. A 97-year-old patient of mine once gave me some good advice. "Never pass up the chance to walk near water," she said. "The ocean, a lake, or a little bubbling brook all have a lesson to teach you. And the most important lessons you'll learn will be about yourself, who you are, what you need, where you're going in life. A nice long walk along the beach will do you more good than any pill."

| ASK FOR AFFECTION |

Praise is well, compliment is well, but affection—that is the last and final and most precious reward that any man can win, whether by character or achievement.
—Mark Twain

Human beings have a deep-rooted need for affection at every stage of their lives. Nearly everyone's familiar with the "failure-to-thrive syndrome" experienced by infants deprived of human touch and cuddling. Little kids exposed to physical or emotional abuse can actually develop growth impairment, called psychosocial dwarfism.

Yet what about mature supposedly well-adjusted adults, successful professionals and executives? Does affection serve as anything other than a pleasant diversion in adulthood? The answer is a resounding yes! A hug, a kiss, or even a friendly pat on the back serve as expressions of affirmation, acceptance, and appreciation. Affection benefits both the giver and the recipient by increasing endorphins and decreasing stress hormones like cortisol and adrenaline. The beneficial effects even extend to affection exchanged between people and their pets. The mere act of petting your puppy or playing with a kitten can reduce pulse rate and blood pressure for an hour or more.

> ## MILLIONS OF ELDERLY PEOPLE ENDURE PROLONGED PERIODS OF AFFECTION DEPRIVATION.

There's no doubt affection does good things for our physiology. Does it have an impact on the aging process? I can't say it's been studied extensively, but I can say I've observed a colossal difference in older patients based on the degree of affection in their lives. Millions of elderly people endure prolonged periods of affection deprivation. Years spent living alone or in a nursing home without so much as a hug or kiss take a terrible toll on body, mind, and spirit. These poor souls lead a far different existence from their more fortunate counterparts who enjoy loving, nurturing relationships throughout their lives.

| LAUGH AT THE LITTLE THINGS |

Laughter is inner jogging.
—Norman Cousins

When I think of all the patients I've cared for over the last 25 years, the "successful agers" all have had a sense of humor and a ready laugh. That's not to suggest they were immune from illness, stress, or strife. On the contrary, many of them were confronted with more than their share of trauma and tragedy.

LAUGHTER MAKES US FEEL GOOD.

The lifeline that saved their sanity was an ability to laugh at the little things.

Numerous studies on the physiologic effects of laughter have demonstrated some remarkable findings. A good sustained belly laugh causes the blood pressure and pulse to rise briefly, but then fall to significantly lower levels for an hour or more. The lungs expand more fully improving oxygenation of the blood. Endorphin production goes up and "stress hormone" production (adrenaline and cortisol) goes down.

All of these findings confirm what we've always known from experience—laughter makes us feel good. So why don't we do it more often? Probably because we're so busy being serious, professional, realistic, and mature. But since being serious, professional, realistic, and mature has not been shown to prolong life or enhance the enjoyment of it; we're probably better off laughing a lot more than we do.

| FABRICATE FUN |

Gladness of the heart is the life of a man and
the joyfulness of a man prolongeth his days.
–Ecclesiasticus 30:22

Did you know that you could actually choose to be cheerful?

I know, it's a radical concept, but our attitude is the only thing we really can control. As a doctor, I appreciate the challenging nature of that statement. Practicing medicine in this day and age is hardly a barrel of fun. But fun is precisely what most of us need. One of the most important questions I ask patients when I take their history is "What do you do for fun?" If they can't fire back an immediate response, I have instant insight into their situation. It's sad to realize how many people hear that question and look at me with a blank stare. They can't even remember the last time they had fun. It's tough to feel joyful when your life is that dull. I admit it takes some effort, especially when you're in a rut, but the best medicine is often having something fun to do in your life.

Of course, fun is a relative term. Depending on your mood, mindset, and level of energy, fun can range from 48 hours of uninterrupted peace and quiet to parasailing along the Pacific coast. The activity is not nearly as important as the degree of joyful anticipation it generates.

I'll never forget the sage advice of a feisty centenarian sharing her secret for happiness, "In all things, give thanks," she said. "No matter what happens it could be worse and it almost always gets better. Let go of the past, make the most of the present and don't worry about the future. Always have something to look forward to. Be gentle with yourself and others. Work hard, hug people, laugh a lot and have fun. It's worked for me," she concluded triumphantly. I have a hunch it would work for us all.

| CELEBRATE SEX |

Love dies only when growth stops.
—Pearl S. Buck

Would it surprise you to learn that your love life can have a major impact on the way you age? It's not exactly a hot topic of conversation on the talk shows. In our culture one rarely hears the words "aging" and "sex" in the same sentence. Not that there's any shortage of information about sex out there, but sexuality in the context of aging is viewed by many as an oxymoron. That's unfortunate since human beings are sexual creatures throughout their life span.

I've often suspected the stumbling block for centuries has been an unbalanced view of healthy human sexuality. Throughout the ages there have been those lofty-minded souls who, in pursuit of spiritual development, have sought to become asexual. Far more common and self-destructive are those

IN OUR CULTURE ONE RARELY HEARS THE WORDS "AGING" AND "SEX" IN THE SAME SENTENCE.

whose obsession with sex have left them dysfunctional in every other aspect of life.

Achieving a healthy, fulfilling, and responsible balance is no small feat given the vagaries of our crazy current culture. But a well-known researcher in the field of successful aging, Dr. Kenneth Pelletier, discovered what might be the best definition of healthy sexuality in happy, healthy older adults.

Dr. Pelletier found that people who looked, felt, and acted much younger than their chronological age had a strong sense of their masculinity or femininity. They had close, loving, nurturing relationships with both sexes. They took good care of themselves and resisted the temptation to "let themselves go." Many of his subjects lived alone, were widowed, or were married but no longer having intercourse. However, they continued to enjoy affection, warmth, and intimacy on other levels. I've encountered the same scenario in my practice. A charming couple in their

> ...THEY STILL HUGGED AND KISSED AND CUDDLED AND HELD HANDS AND HAD CANDLELIGHT DINNERS.

eighties confided that although they hadn't had sex in 15 years, they still hugged and kissed and cuddled and held hands and had candlelight dinners. I know folks in their twenties who would settle for as much.

Despite decades of misguided, destructive, irresponsible portrayals of sex in the media, human sexuality is still a wonderful, mysterious, revitalizing gift. Without the full expression of our masculinity or femininity we become virtual androids existing in an emotional vacuum. And that's not a happy way to go through life. Men and women should be equal but different. It's that difference that makes life interesting and worthy of celebration. As the French say, "Vive la difference!"

| AIM FOR ADVENTURE |

Far better it is to dare mighty things, to win glorious triumphs even though checkered by failure, than to rank with those poor spirits who neither enjoy nor suffer much because they live in the gray twilight that knows neither victory nor defeat.
—Theodore Roosevelt

Have you dared any mighty things lately? Or do you live in the gray twilight of boredom? I've yet to read about it in the

New England Journal of Medicine but personal observation has convinced me that people can literally bore themselves to death. I witness the phenomenon almost daily in hospital and nursing home settings. But millions of people in every age group and in otherwise good health drift aimlessly in a sea of boredom oblivious to the realization they have a choice. The classic example is the recently retired professional or business man, who, after a few months of golfing, fishing, and watching Wheel of Fortune finds dwindling levels of satisfaction and enjoyment in his new found leisure. It's a rare individual who can take pride in being "another old retired guy." But the workplace doesn't prepare us for the obscurity, anonymity, and boredom of a poorly planned retirement.

No doubt it's possible to develop exciting new interests at any age. Yet it's far better (and infinitely more fun) to develop the habit of pursuing new interests and adventures. Adventure, by definition, requires some action that's out of the ordinary, a break from routine. It stretches our comfort zone, which is precisely why many people avoid it like the plague. Of course, adventure is a relative term. A diehard daredevil may be bored

EVEN PINT-SIZED ADVENTURES CAN BE IMMENSELY BENEFICIAL.

with anything less thrilling than hang-gliding over Victoria Falls, while the couch potato accustomed to wearing the hair off the back of his head may find a trip to a different grocery store unnerving.

Even pint-sized adventures can be immensely beneficial. The point is to get your juices flowing and stimulate a few new synaptic connections in your brain. It's fun. It's an excellent excuse to learn Italian. And it's one of the most important secrets of "successful agers."

| REFERENCES |

* **Disease Prevention in Aging Adults**
Health Aging: Preventing Disease and Improving Quality of Life Among Older Americans. CDC publication. www.cdc.gov/nccdphp/aag/aag_aging.htm

* **Physical Activity and Aging**
Burke G, Arnold A, Bild D et al. Factors associated with healthy aging: the cardiovascular health study. *J Am Geriatr Soc.* 2001; 49 (3): 254–62.

DiPietro L. Physical activity in aging: changes in patterns and their relationship to health and function. *J Gerontol A Biol Sci Med Sci.* 2001; 56 Spec No 2 (2): 13–22.

* **Mind and Memory in Aging**
Linney B. How to be viewed as a sage in your elder years. *Physician Exec.* 1999; 25 (2)L 68–70.

Khalsa D. Integrated medicine and the prevention and reversal of memory loss. *Alt Ther Health Med.* 1998 Nov; 4 (6): 38–43.

* **Sexuality and Aging**
National Institute on Aging publication. AgePage. Sexuality in Later Life. www.niapublications.org/engagepages/sexuality.asp

* **Antioxidants and Aging**
National Institute on Aging publication. AgePage. Life Extension: Science Fact or Science Fiction? www.niapublications.org/engagepages/lifeext.asp.

* Mood and Depression in Aging Adults

Achat H, Kawachi I, Spiro A 3rd. Optimism and depression as predictors of physical and mental health functioning; the Normative Aging Study. *Ann Behav Med.* 2000; 22 (2): 127–30.

Levy B, Slade M, Kasl S. Longitudinal benefit of positive self-perceptions of aging on functional health. *J Gerontol B Psychol Sci Soc Sci.* 2002; 57 (5): 409–17.

* Spirituality and Cardiovascular Disease

Aviles J, Whelan S, Hernke D. Intercessory prayer and cardiovascular disease progression in a coronary care unit population: a randomized controlled trial. *Mayo Clinic Proc.* 2001; 76 (12): 1192–8.

Morris E. The relationship of spirituality to coronary heart disease. *Altern Ther Health Med.* 2001; 7 (5): 96–98.

* Forgiveness and Health

Lawler K, Younger J, Piferi R et al. A change of heart: cardiovascular correlates of forgiveness in response to interpersonal conflict. *J Behav Med.* 2003; 26 (5): 373–93.